The Institute of African American Psychology

(IAAP)

"Using psychological science to create equal opportunities for achieving the American Dream."

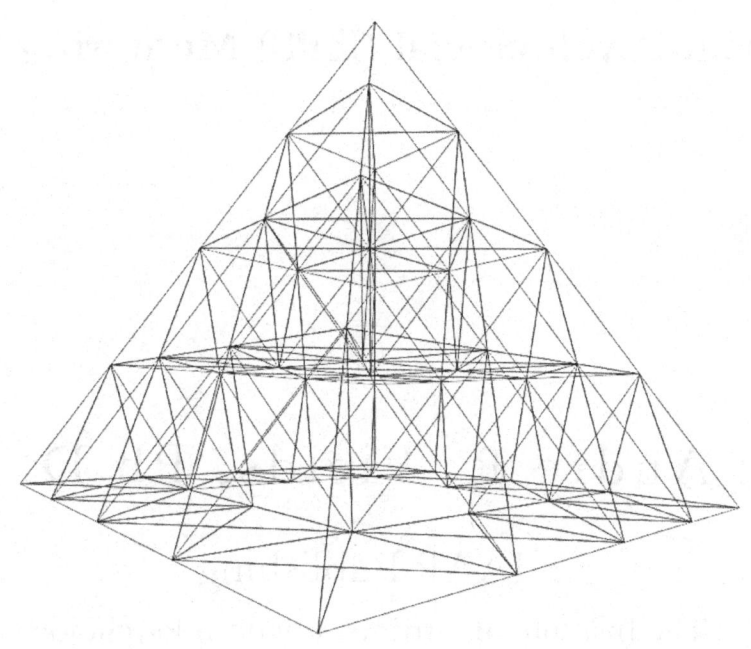

MENTORING BLACK MALE STUDENTS
One Step at a Time
The 55 Golden Rules

The EduPsychoSocial (EPS) Mentoring Model
A Mentoring Framework for Empowering and Educating Black Male Students

Andre R. Fields, Ph.D.

IAAP Publishing

The Institute of African American Psychology

IAAP Publishing

FOR INFORMATION:

IAAP Publishing
PHONE: 616.323.8506
EMAIL: **afields@theiaap.org**
WEBSITE: www.theiaap.org

Mentoring Black Male Students
One Step at a Time
The 55 Golden Rules

The EduPsychoSocial Mentoring Model

Copyright © 2016 by Andre R. Fields

All rights reserved. Printed in the United States of America.

No part of this book may be reproduced, stored, or transmitted in any form or by any means without prior written permission from the publisher except in the case of brief quotations embodied in critical articles or reviews.

Special discounts on bulk quantities are available.

For information contact: www.theiaap.org

Cover Design: Piper Adonya
www.piperadonya.com

Printed in the United States of America

A catalog record of this book is available from the Library of Congress.

ISBN-13: 978-0692839645 (IAAP)

ISBN-10: 069283964X

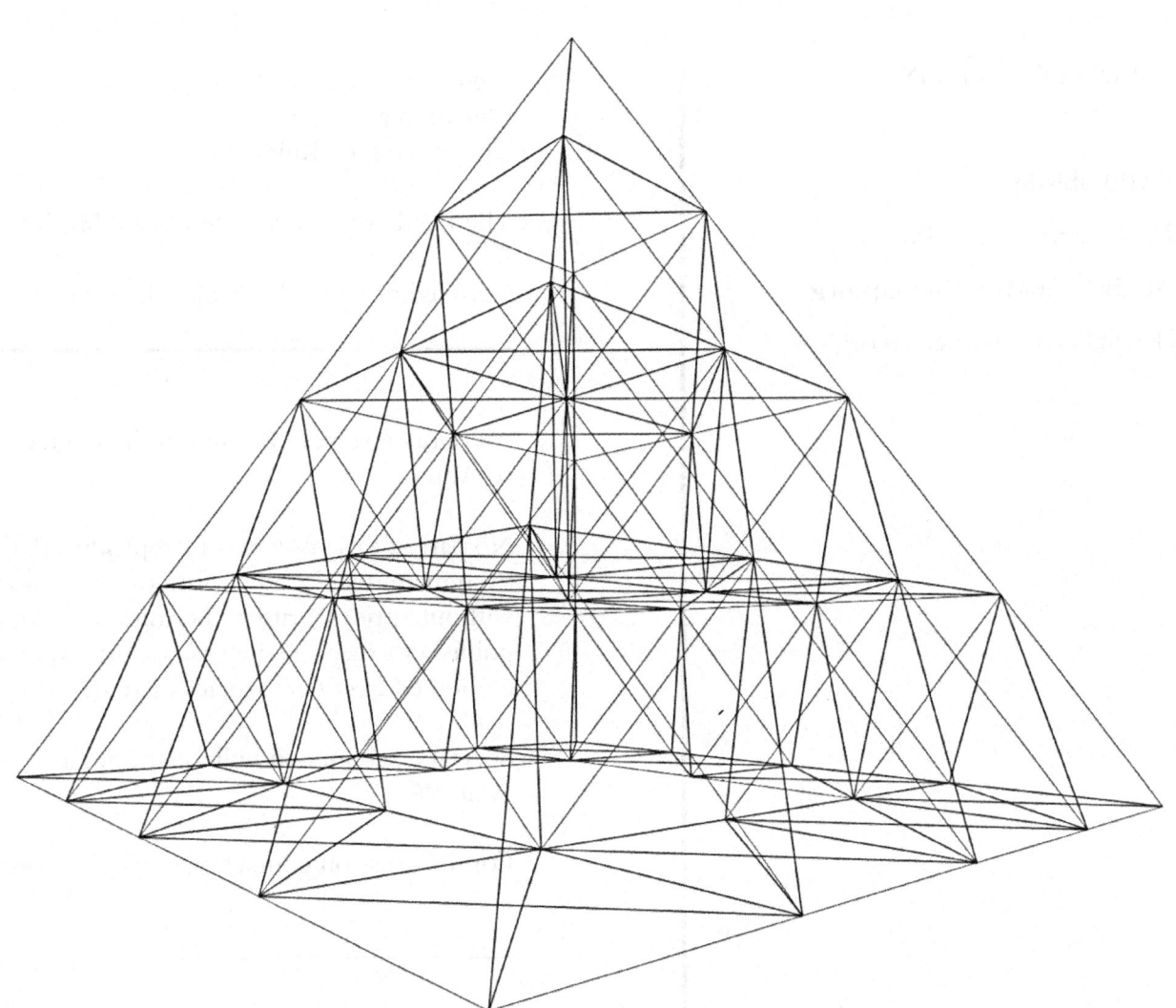

MENTORING BLACK MALE STUDENTS
One Step at a Time
The 55 Golden Rules

The EduPsychoSocial (EPS) Mentoring Model
A Mentoring Framework for Empowering and Educating Black Male Students

SECTION I.
Understanding Racially-Contextualized Mentoring

SECTION II.
The Social Engineering of Black Male Failure

SECTION III.
How Educational Systems Fail Black Male Students

SECTION IV.
The Goals and Processes of Racially-Contextualized Mentoring

SECTION V.
Identifying and Minimizing Risks

Dear Heroes,

It takes a skill-set to build a skill-set. In order for a mentor to effectively impact his Black male mentee, he has to have a working knowledge base that informs his conceptualization of the Black male experience. As a school psychologist and director of a racially-contextualized leadership development program, I have spent thousands of hours case managing the educational journeys of Black male college students. During this time I have been able to observe, research, organize, and catalog the educational, institutional, social, and psychological experiences of the Black male college student.

The depth of qualitative data I have gathered during this time of advising, mentoring, and counseling these students has been personally ground breaking as it has afforded me the opportunity to identify the common threats, risks, and barriers Black males encounter on their educational paths. Over the course of my experiences I have also been able to identify common approaches and mentoring modalities that effectively build into Black males the psychological skill-set necessary to "do" college.

As a result of intense and frequent interactions with Black male college students, I have been afforded the opportunity to use qualitative data to strategically develop, expand, and enhance a race-based mentoring framework. This framework is contextualized around the psychosocial experiences of the Black male college student. This mentoring framework was researched and developed with the deepest considerations of the characteristics, personality traits, mannerisms, attitudes, and psychological posturings that are most predictive of academic failure as well as academic success.

The purpose of this manual is to assist mentors gain a deeper understanding of the intersection of race, racism, and Black male underachievement. This manual provides vantage points, philosophies, and approaches mentors can incorporate when working with Black males. This manual also outlines the common psychological, educational, social, and institutional risks Black males are most likely to encounter. The short-term longitudinal data that I have been able to collect and analyze has provided me with a big picture view of the national crisis of Black male underachievement. It is my greatest hope that the information in this manual will empower mentors, institutions, and organizations around the country in their efforts to educate and empower the Black males they serve.

Andre "Dr. Dre" Fields, Ph.D.

To all the fathers, uncles, sons, and cousins who decided to help someone else's baby.

SECTION I.

Understanding Racially-Contextualized Mentoring

MENTORING BLACK MALE STUDENTS
One Step at a Time

There is Something in the Water
The Profoundly Complex Epidemic of Black Male Failure

In the most recent decades, there has been a spiraling national trend of social and academic underachievement on the part of Black males. Specifically, there are striking disparities between the rates of academic failings, unemployment, and poverty amongst Black males and other comparable male groups spread across the American landscape. This current and seemingly persistent pattern of negative life outcomes amongst Black males has become a profoundly difficult American issue. The reality of this "national emergency" warrants an intentional effort by educators to purposefully implement contextualized curricular models and culturally-appropriate teaching modalities that will psychologically empower Black males and reverse this population's trend of academic underachievement.

The EduPsychoSocial (EPS) Mentoring Framework
A Psychosocial Framework for Mentoring Black Male Students

The EPS Theory of Causation
Race-Specific Social Experiences = Race-Specific Psychological Issues = Race-Specific Educational Outcomes

During the adolescent stage of human growth and development teens are tasked with developing an identity. In these formative years, adolescents experience tumultuous emotions, distorted perceptions, and confusing biological changes. Throughout this stage of psychological sensitivity and emotional vulnerability, Black males are systematically indoctrinated by an ideology that propagates the notion that Black males are inferior, incapable, and essentially a national liability. Research has consistently demonstrated that Black male adolescents are targeted for social stigma more than any other category of American citizen. Sadly and consequently, at a very early age, Black males understand that the world views them, because of their appearance, through a perpetual lens of negativity and repulsion.

This consistent pattern of inferiorizing communication comes during a time when young maturing minds lack the psychological sophistication, life experience, and brain development required to engage in the level of critical thinking necessary to guard against the internalization of these negative messages. This absence of an effective psychological defense system in the face of a relentless and unavoidable stigmatizing messaging system leads to destructive internalization and the ultimate construction of a failure schema.

At all points of the formative years, the egocentric adolescent brain believes that life and the world revolves around him and he is on the world's stage being judged, critiqued, and defined. Throughout this profoundly impressionable stage, Black boys are being tragically racialized and stigmatized to the point that the internalization of inferiority is inevitable. In the end, we as a society, are left to pick up the tab on the cost of underperformance from a category of American citizens who were socially engineered for failure.

Note: If you put 100 White boys through these same stigmatic psyche-shaping experiences they would achieve the same statistical results.

In a World of Trouble
A Rationale for the EPS Framework

Racism is fundamentally defined as the internal belief that one race is superior to another race. According to research, Black males are the most stigmatized portion of the American population. This means that Black males are essentially incapable of escaping or avoiding routine exposures to inferiorizing messages and interactions. Beginning with a blank slate, the building blocks of the Black male's Belief System (belief about self, life, and future), Value System (what matters, what he is personally responsible for, and what is respectable), and Self-System (personal sense of efficacy, esteem, and image) are based on stigma and rejection. These building blocks of stigma and rejection become infrastructures of hopelessness which evolve into a jaded Belief System (internally or externally incapable of attaining the American Dream), a socially ineffective Value System (misguided motivations) and a disempowered Self-System (no power, no value, and no dignity).

The EPS framework is guided by the principle that the Belief, Value, and Self-System work together to determine perception and that perception ultimately determines one's response system. With this in mind, it can be theorized that as a result of destructive internalization, Black boys psychologically evolve into Black men who perceive themselves, the world, life, and the future through a perceptual lens of negativity, rejection, and alienation. Ultimately, in the face of situations or challenges that require hope, the hopeless Black male is statistically more likely to respond with maladaptive coping, escapism, avoidance, and self-sabotage. In the spirit of this theory and reasoning, the immediate goal of the EPS Mentoring Model is to re-condition, re-engineer, re-build, and re-program the Belief-System, Value-System, and Self-System of the Black male.

The American Education System
A National Disaster

Currently, the American education system lacks the capacity to pick up enough pieces of the fragmented Black male to improve his chances of achieving academic success. The American education system needs to make an intentional effort to provide contextualized learning environments (culturally appropriate information, people, ideas, support, resources, social networks, etc.). Such contextualized learning environments are much more capable of building the psychological skill-set required for sustained engagement with the process of being educated (hope, motivation, impulse control, delayed gratification, confidence, etc.). Until these sweeping modifications are made, the American education system will never have the capacity to educate Black males. High schools and college campuses play a significant role in psyche-shaping and identity development. With this in mind, educational systems should make it a professional and moral obligation to provide Black males with a learning environment capable of fostering positive development and reversing the Black male's trajectory towards academic failure.

The EPS Mentoring Intervention
A Social Miracle!

National Stigma and Systemic Discrimination have resulted in deep histories of rejection, alienation, and unmet socio-emotional needs for Black males. These harsh developmental experiences necessitate an affirming mentoring relationship that intentionally considers the race-specific needs of young Black males.

The EPS Mentoring Model strives to reverse the impact of these negative developmental experiences by providing Black males with a relational learning platform for experiencing positive young adulthood experiences. These positive young adult experiences are delivered via a Black male's engagement in a structured, stable, and sustained relationship with a valued and respected mentor. Simply put, the purpose of this mentoring relationship is to "bring out the best" in the Black male mentee.

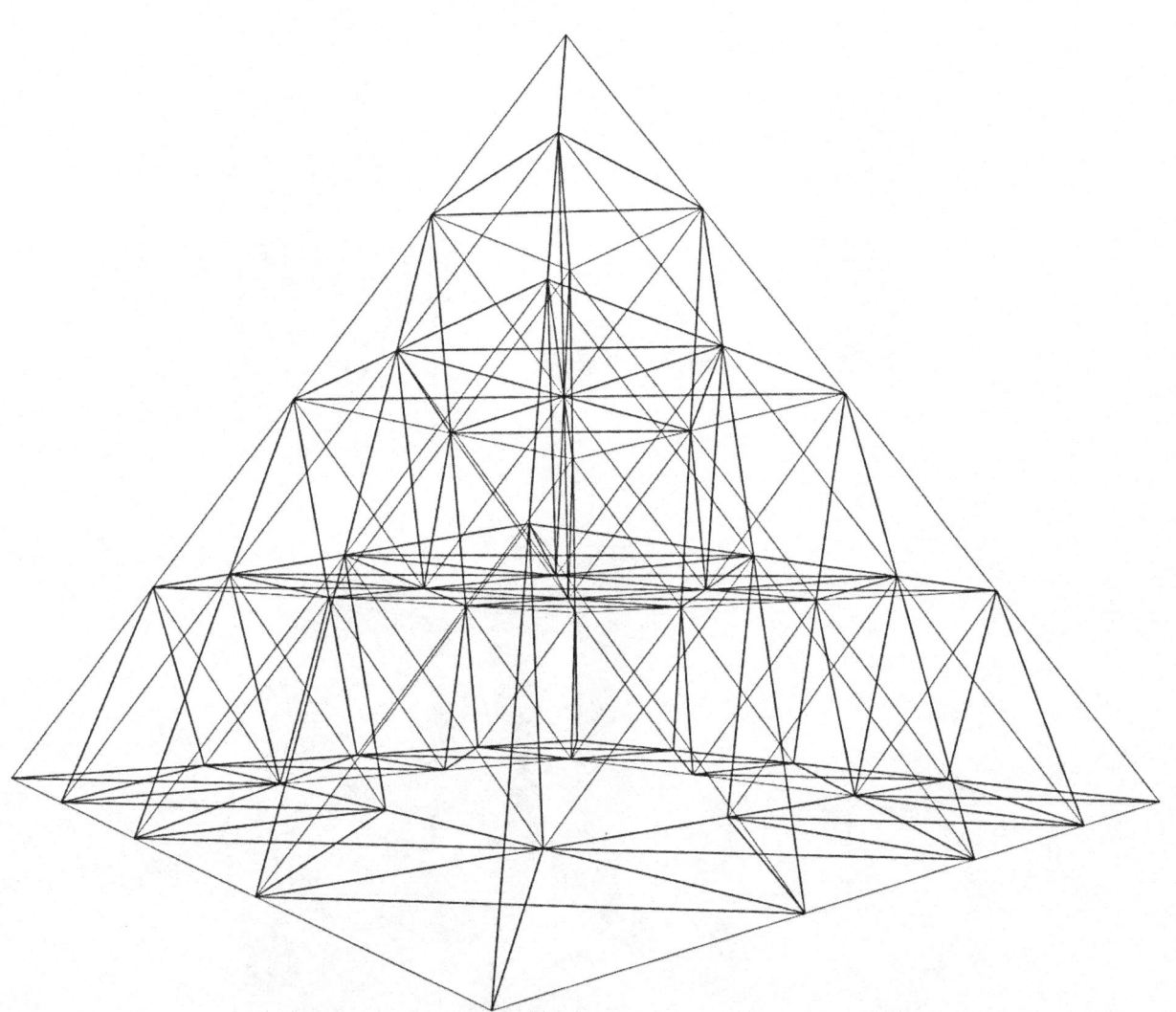

GOLDEN RULE 1

Science Trumps Tradition: Racial-Contextualization Works

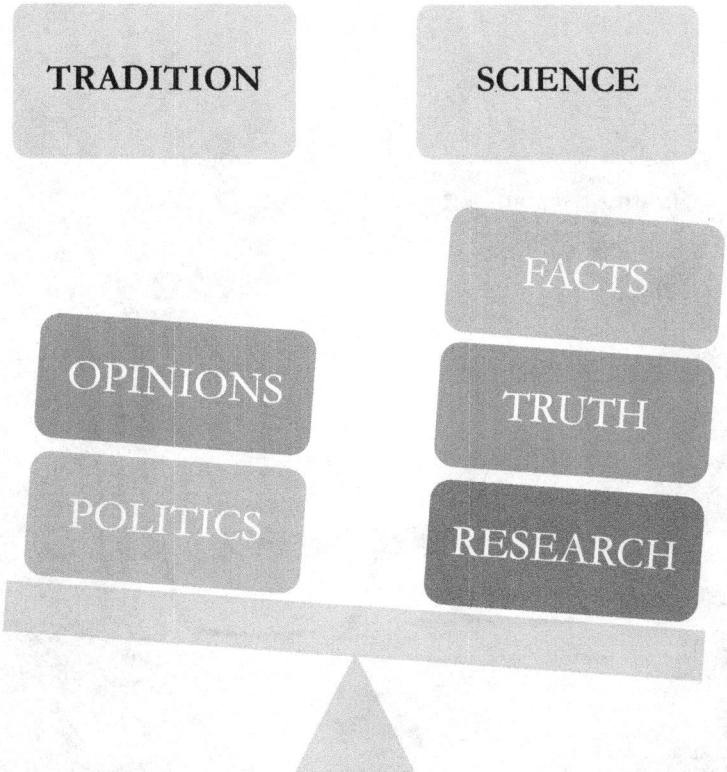

Those who are racially-insensitive assume that all students should be educated with the same teaching modaities and achieve the same level of academic achievement. This assumption comes from the seat of White privilege. Those with Majority privilege lack an awareness of the race-specific social experiences of Black male students. Racially-insensitive individuals admit that, yes Black males have less opportunities and resources, but yet in the same breath these individuals will say Black males should not receive even the smallest amount of specialized resource allocation to catch up to other citizens, who by social default, had more opportunities from birth. It is not necessarily the EPS philosophy that extra monies and allocations be spent on supplementing the Black male struggle. It is however, the EPS' strongest position that a fair and equal amount of resources be spent on creating racially-contextualized teaching and mentoring modalities that have been proven through practice and/or research to effectively empower and educate Black males.

GOLDEN RULE 2

Relational Learning. The Secret Ingredient.

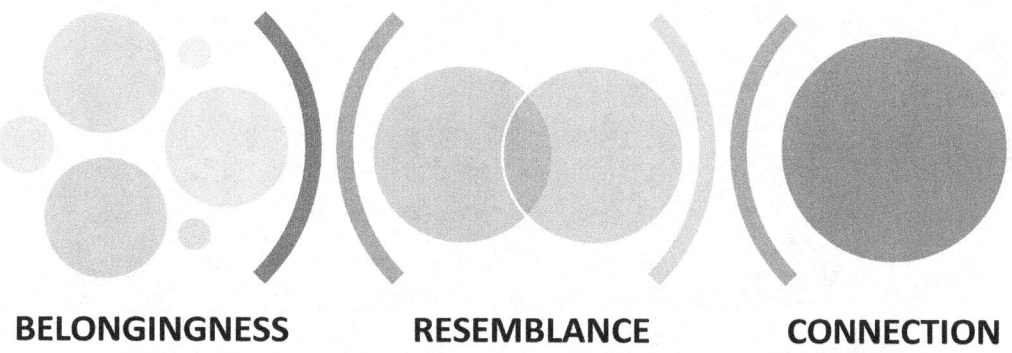

BELONGINGNESS   **RESEMBLANCE**   **CONNECTION**

There are numerous methods and modalities across the nation attempting improve the academic performance of Black male students. Of all these approaches, relational learning has been consistently proven to successfully move the needle on Black male achievement. Relational learning is the process of engaging Black male students in stable and genuine interactions with credible, knowledgeable, and respectable mentors. This stable and genuine relationship serves as an instrument for educating and empowering Black male students. Relational learning utilizes human relationships to enhance learning efficiency by fostering a sense of belonging and connectedness that eventually triggers optimal learning and increased inspiration.

Racially-contextualized mentoring acknowledges the fact that people discover, understand, and express themselves through the lens of their race, culture, gender, religion, etc. Qualitative data has uncovered that racially-contextualized relational learning (via mentoring) is primarily responsible for the majority of the positive outcomes produced by the EPS framework. This makes sense if you consider the fact that Black males are the most socially rejected portion of the American population. It makes even more sense if you consider the fact that Black children are the most likely category of children to be raised in fatherless homes.

GOLDEN RULE 3

Power in Numbers!

What is Mentoring?

- A *healthy relationship* in which a Black male student has access to the information and inspiration needed to achieve optimal levels of personal, social, educational, and professional development. This racially-appropriate relational learning experience provides the student with access to the information and inspiration he will need to overcome *race-related social barriers, insitutional barriers, learning struggles, economic challenges, internalized stigma, and a destructive self-system (esteem, efficacy, and image).*

The EPS Mentoring Model for of educating and empowering Black males views relational learning as the primary component for building into Black male's the psychological skill-set necessary for completing the educational process. In a relational learning scenario, the primary role of the mentor is to serve as a type of knowledge source for students to access information related to their personal, social, educational, and professional development. Mentoring is not a "talking at" or "lecturing" activity. In stark contrast, a mentoring relationship is an enriching conversational learning process built upon instructional interactions and empowering encounters between a student and a respected and consistent role-figure/role-model.

GOLDEN RULE 4

Mentors are…bring…do…

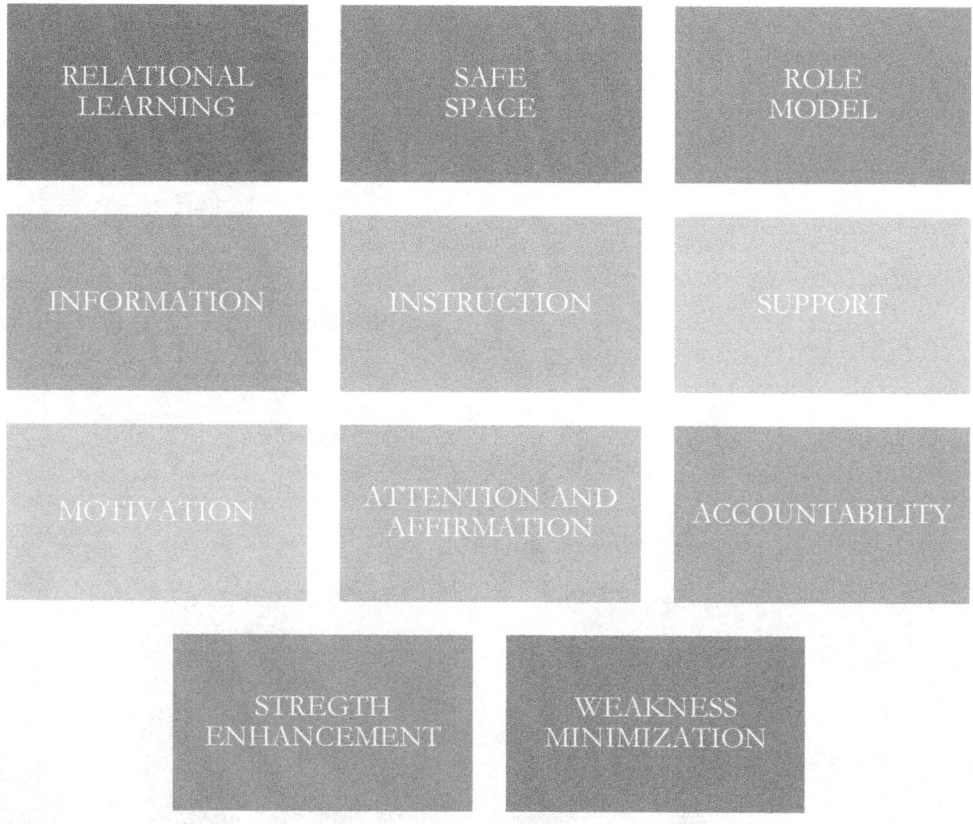

Mentors have the job of being external forces of inspiration. Beyond inspiration, mentors serve as developmental crutches. This role of providing developmental support based on the educational, social, and psychological needs of the student must be steady and remain in place until the student's risk factors have been resolved or the student has acquired the internal fortitude or external protective factors necessary to minimize the impact of an identified risk.

Mentors facilitate a healthy relationship that effectively "brings out the best" in a Black male student. This bringing out of the best is accomplished via the consistent and sequential delivery of affirmation, relational accountability`, elevated expectations, reliable support, weakness-management, strength-utilization, role-modeling, and a safe relational space to communicate frustrations, fears, victories, etc.

GOLDEN RULE 5

Preferred Coaching Characteristics

- Vision Casting and Hope Building
- Strength Finding and Resource Matching
- Genuineness and Respect
- Expectation and Accountability
- Challenge and Support

There is a seemingly infinite amount of available techniques and approaches that can be utilized in a mentoring relationship. Despite a wide range of mentoring techniques, there appears to be several relational learning conditions and mentor characteristics necessary in order for impactful mentoring to take place. EPS research has uncovered that the majority of change generated through the mentoring process, is mediated by 5 key mentoring conditions. The 5 key coaching conditions that make up the EPS Mentoring Model are:

1. Vision Casting and Hope Building
2. Strength Finding and Resource Matching
3. Genuineness and Respect
4. Expectation and Accountability
5. Challenge and Support

GOLDEN RULE 6

Vision Casting and Hope Building

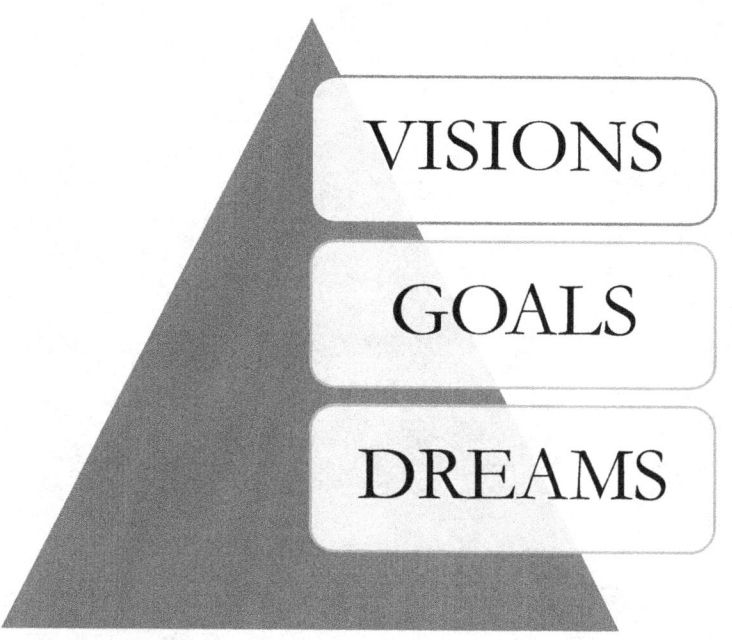

Due to deep histories of stigma and disappointment many Black males have been stripped of their ability to *Dream*. An immediate responsibility of the EPS guided mentor is to provide mentees with an opportunity to map out their *Life Goals*. By providing a mentee with the opportunity to map out or script his future, you are moving him out of the daydreaming phase and into the action phase of the vision building process. Once a *Vision* is outlined, it will serve as a constant reminder to the student that he needs to make decisions that will maximize his chances of accomplishing his life goals.

The EPS method of mentoring sees the mentoring relationship as a great platform for vision and hope building. In this relationship, a mentor serves as a type of co-pilot helping the student navigate his way towards his vision while hopefully minimizing his chances of "losing his way". As an assistant vision-caster, the mentor is effectively training a student to not only want success but to also believe that success is possible. As a mentor, it is pivotal that hope in the future is constantly being re-generated. A mentor must relentlessly re-calibrate his student's thinking and behaving towards his desired future reality. Such hope re-generation and vision re-enforcement will minimize a student's chances of giving up on the educational process.

GOLDEN RULE 7
Strength Finding and Resource Matching

An effective mentor is intentional about not placing a priority on the psychological shortcomings of the student. In contrast, an effective mentor will endeavor to focus on what strengths and resources the student already has at his disposal. Effective mentoring relationships naturally activate a student's internal strengths. These internal strengths are "translated" into the world of academia and utilized as weapons for overcoming life challenges. Internal strengths (i.e. psychological resources) include persistence, openness, faith, optimism, hope, readiness for change, and personal responsibility. External resources include the people, processes, supports, and services that can increase a student's capacity for overcoming life challenges.

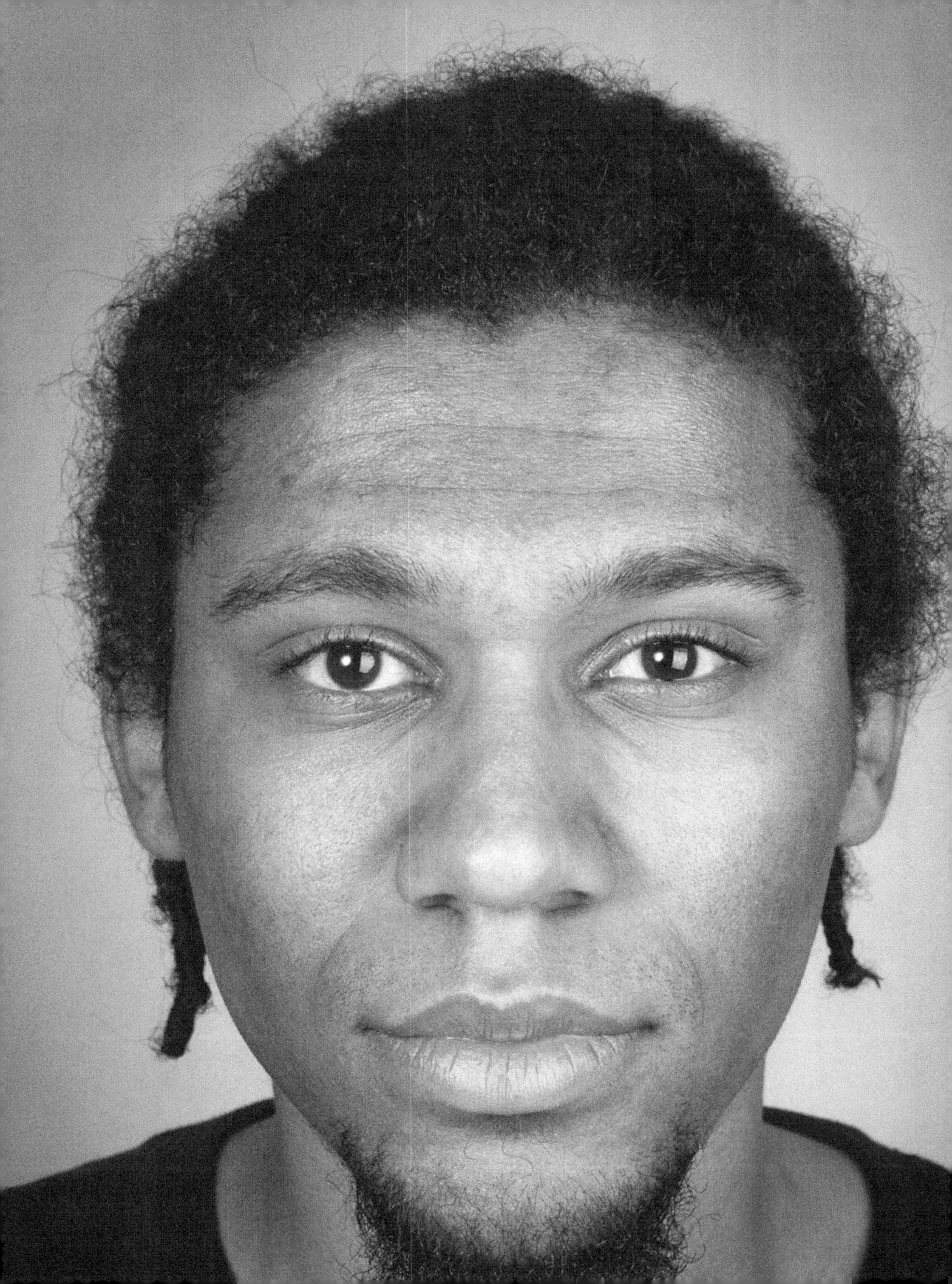

GOLDEN RULE 8

Genuineness and Respect

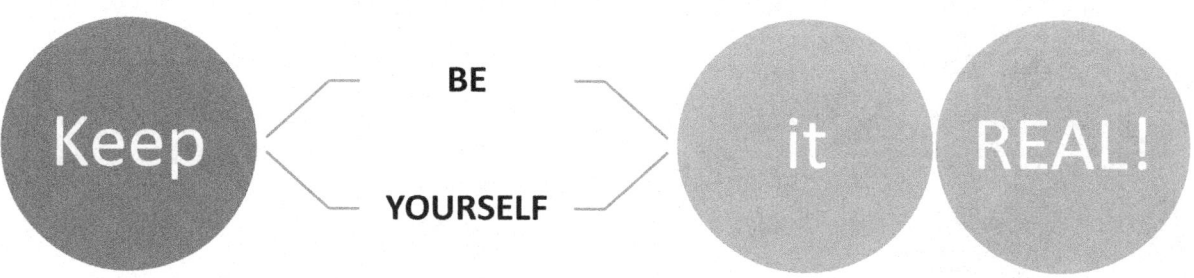

The information and inspiration transmitted via the mentoring relationship serves as a master switch for engaging the gears of academic success. A student's inherent strengths and abilities can be effectively triggered when he is engaged in a warm, genuine, respectful, accepting, and empathetic relationship with a mentor. In a mentoring relationship, genuine and sincere interaction serve as operational bridges of relational communication that build rapport, trust, and comradery. Once genuineness and sincerity build the bridge of trust, rapport, comradery thought shaping, morale boosting, and life-changing communication can take place. Essentially, a mentor serves as a type of link of relational communication that mediates the connection between the Black male student and academic success. EPS guided mentors enhance their mentoring effects by carefully integrating relationship-building dialogues and behaviors into their mentoring sessions.

GOLDEN RULE 9

Expectation and Accountability

The purpose of expectation is to guide decision-making. Expectations also determine a person's level of personal effort and investment. In the very early stages of the mentoring relationship, mentors and mentees work together to mutually establish clearly defined social and academic expectations. This definitive outline of expectations works to provide a student with concrete measures of accomplishment and accountability. As it relates to expectations and accountability, mentors serve as a mirror of duty and responsibility, reflecting back to the student their personal obligation to be accountable for their actions and give an answer for any behavior incongruent with established expectations. Routine exposure to mentoring exchanges that consistently reinforce expectations, serve as a strong voice of accountability which will empower the student to consistently invest the level of energy, focus, and dedication necessary to achieve their educational goals.

GOLDEN RULE 10
Challenge and Support

The primary purpose of the mentoring relationship is to promote positive personal, social, and educational growth. Positive growth cannot be achieved without a balanced psychological interplay of challenge and support within an established mentoring relationship. By serving as a major source of uncompromising challenge and unyielding support, mentors build personal responsibility while providing external aid.

Specifically, a mentor serves as a type of "human lesson plan" in that he is downloading into his mentee a specific base of life-knowledge he has acquired over the course of his life. This base of life-knowledge serves as an instrument for challenging disempowering thoughts, dysfunctional expressions, misguided values, and counterproductive behaviors. At the same time, mentors serve as a psychosocial support system in that they use their base of life-knowledge as a type of developmental crutch to support the student as he stumbles along his educational path. As a mentee is continually challenged and supported by his mentor's "life curriculum", he will begin to remember, internalize, and utilize the perspectives, principles, and practices his mentor once used to overcome life obstacles and complete the educational process.

GOLDEN RULE 11

Appreciation of the Student's Culture = Effective Affirmation

- Black Culture
- Black Expression
- Black Dialect
- Black Identity
- Black Physical Characteristics
- Black History

The Black Experience

It is critical for a mentor to display genuine appreciation for the Black American experience. Mentors who respect the history, cultural expressions, dialects, and physical characteristics of Black Americans will have a much easier time building trust and rapport with their Black male students. Again, in order for the mentor's role to be impactful, genuine appreciation of the student's culture and race must be communicated. This genuine cultural appreciation is typically more easily and naturally communicated by Black American mentors. This does not mean non-Black staff, faculty, or mentors are incapable of communicating sincere appreciation and respect for the Black experience. This just means it is typically easier to communicate an experience - *you have experienced*. Finally, genuine appreciation must also be communicated by the institution through the strategic construction of a learning environment that uses Black American culture, expression, history, etc. as external sources of motivation.

GOLDEN RULE 12
A Place to Call Home

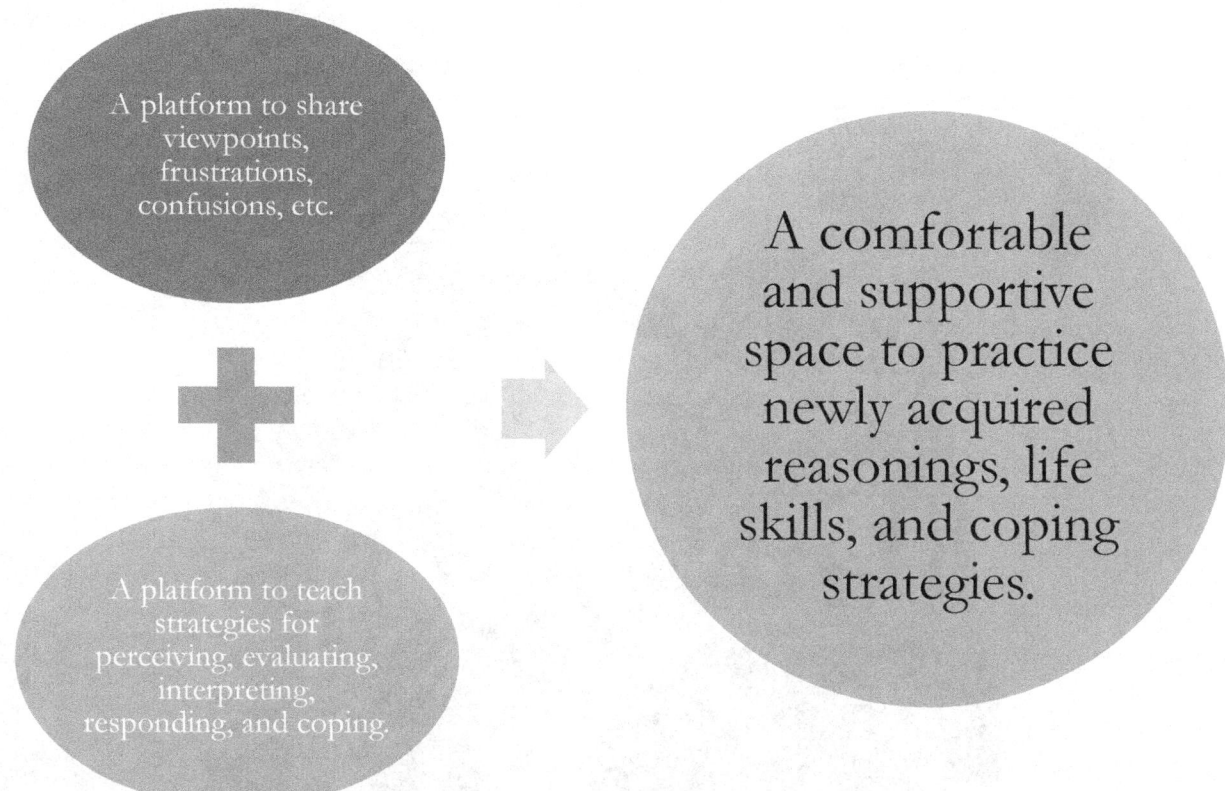

The EPS Mentoring Model views relational learning as a space for comfortable, yet challenging dialogues and interactions to take place. These mediums of empowering communication serve as a relational space for Black males to share their viewpoints, frustrations, confusions, and struggles with a sincerely concerned individual. Because of established rapport, mentors have the legitimate capacity to challenge, confront, and help modify any faulty thinking and/or behaving that may be sabotaging a mentee's academic success.

This relational platform serves as a space where a Black male student can learn new strategies for perceiving, evaluating, interpreting, and ultimately responding to race-related challenges, learning challenges, and any other life challenge in which consultation from a mentor is needed. This relational space also serves as a safe place where a Black male mentee can practice and modify newly acquired life-skills he is seeking to master.

GOLDEN RULE 13

3 Dimensions of Mentoring

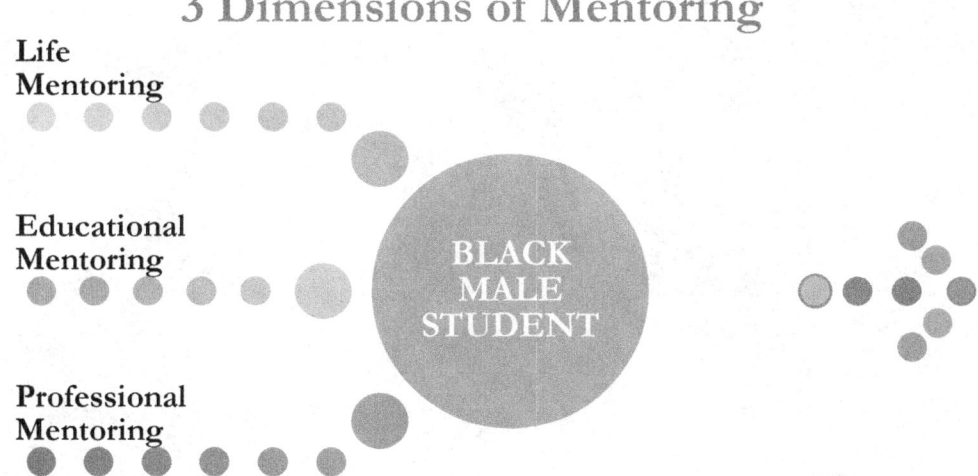

The EPS Mentoring Model divides student mentoring into 3 categories: 1. Life Mentoring, 2. Educational Mentoring and, 3. Professional Mentoring. The EPS Mentoring Model utilizes staff and faculty coaches with the driving philosophy that these Black males have successfully completed the process of finishing college and are thriving in the professional arena all while overcoming general and race-related life issues. This track record of success validates the notion that such individuals have valuable information to transfer to the typical Black male college student.

The EPS Mentoring Model also utilizes student mentors and community mentors to accomplish its goals of educating and empowering Black male students. Student mentors are utilized because of their ability to provide mentees with an "in the trenches" vantage point regarding what it takes to achieve academic success. Student mentors are selected because of their demonstrated strong academic abilities and consistent displays of leadership. This history of academic success combined with strong leadership capabilities are indicative of a student mentor who possess critical information and strategies for success that they may be able to transfer to the typical Black male student. The EPS Mentoring Model utilizes community mentors with the driving philosophy that these individuals represent community members who have attained considerable professional, political, social, or economic success and thus they have invaluable information to disseminate to Black male students.

GOLDEN RULE 14
Holistic Contextualization

- Contextualized around the psychosocial experiences of Black males.
- Holistically contextualized interventions that balance risks and supports.
- Contextualized motivational cues (culture, race, gender, religion, etc.).

A mentoring relationship that seeks to empower and educate Black male students has to go beyond a cookie-cutter or universal approach to mentoring. To engage Black males with a cookie-cutter mentoring experience is to engage this student in a relational learning experience in which only restricted learning can occur.

Because of their race-specific experiences, Black males require race-specific mentoring approaches and learning environments. A mentoring relationship that does not acknowledge the unique Black male experience will be ineffective especially with "super" high risk Black males (i.e. Black males who have internalized National Stigma). Such Black males are the highest risk category of student any mentor, advisor, or instructor will encounter on a college campus.

Institutions of higher learning that utilize mentoring services have to intentionally consider the culture-specific barriers, challenges, and experiences of their Black male population. This deliberate approach will enhance the ability of any institution to address a student's "real problems" and subsequently provide "real solutions".

GOLDEN RULE 15
Race-Based Conceptualization

Race-appropriate conceptualization of the Black male experience.

Race-based conceptualizations on the cause, nature, and trajectory of Black male issues.

In a mentoring relationship, conceptualization can be defined as a mentor's personal assumptions about the causes, triggers, exasperators, and maintainers of a mentee's institutional, learning, social, psychological, and life issues. An EPS guided mentor has to function with a race-appropriate conceptualization of the Black male experience. By doing this the mentor is placing himself in a prime position to appropriately understand the cause, nature, and trajectory of Black male failure. The components that make up a mentor's conceptualization of his Black male mentee should be culturally, racially, and socially considerate. Without properly capturing and conceptualizing the intersection between the Black male experience and Black male failure, a mentor will tragically minimize his ability to appropriately inform, instruct, and inspire his Black male mentee.

GOLDEN RULE 16

Past, Present, and Future: Time Sensitive Mentoring

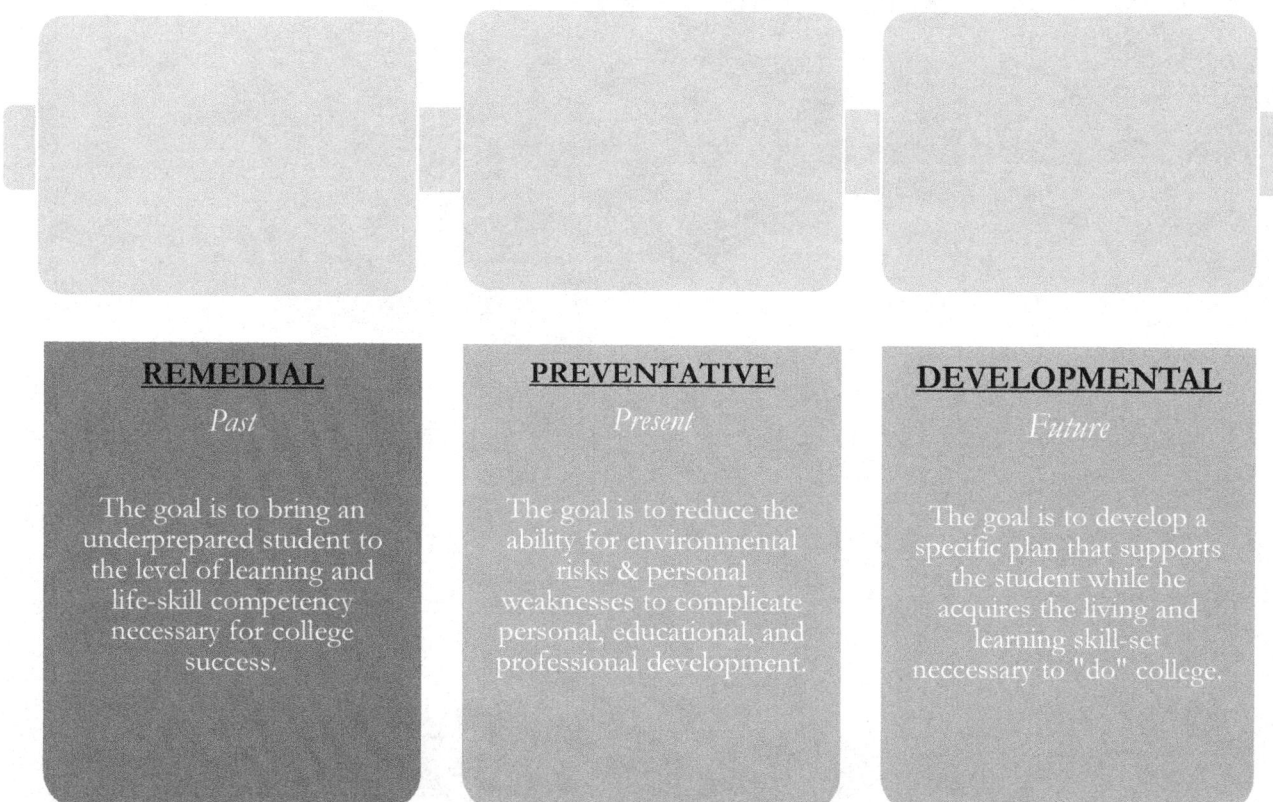

REMEDIAL
Past

The goal is to bring an underprepared student to the level of learning and life-skill competency necessary for college success.

PREVENTATIVE
Present

The goal is to reduce the ability for environmental risks & personal weaknesses to complicate personal, educational, and professional development.

DEVELOPMENTAL
Future

The goal is to develop a specific plan that supports the student while he acquires the living and learning skill-set neccessary to "do" college.

In order to effectively see the big picture of a mentee's educational maze, mentors have to walk one-step behind, one-step ahead, and shoulder to shoulder with their mentees. This big picture vantage point helps the mentor more appropriately detect when to serve as a protector, guide, and/or support based on the immediate needs of the mentee. A good mentor also makes certain to use this big picture perspective as a framework for determining what specific preventative skills need to be acquired or strengthened in order to protect the mentee from his internal and external risks. Finally, effective mentors provide their mentees concrete developmental goals while simultaneously providing them with concrete and specific developmental supports. This developmental support manifests itself through a mentor's utilization of conversation, affirmation, resource matching, and advocacy. This support will guide and nurture the personal growth and development of the Black male student.

GOLDEN RULE 17

What does Holistic Mentoring Look Like?

- Confronting belief systems, values systems, self systems, and dysfunctional coping strategies.
- Addressing inadequate learning strategies.

HOLISTIC MENTORING

- Teaching and modeling how to tolerate stress, cope with barriers, and manage uncomfortable thoughts and emotions.
- Teaching and modeling alternative coping behaviors, productive communication, and emotional expression.

Holistic mentoring is intentionally intrusive when it comes to confronting the Belief-Systems, Value-Systems, and Self-Systems that complicate a Black male's ability to "do" college. Furthermore, a holistic mentoring approach is strategic about addressing the inadequate learning strategies his mentee may be utilizing in and out of the classroom. The EPS guided mentor must deliberately teach and model effective approaches for managing stress, life barriers, relationships, uncomfortable emotions, etc. By teaching and modeling alternative coping behaviors, holistic mentoring places Black male students on a path towards academic success at a much higher rate than Black male students who are not actively involved in a holistic mentoring relationship.

GOLDEN RULE 18
Positive College Experiences

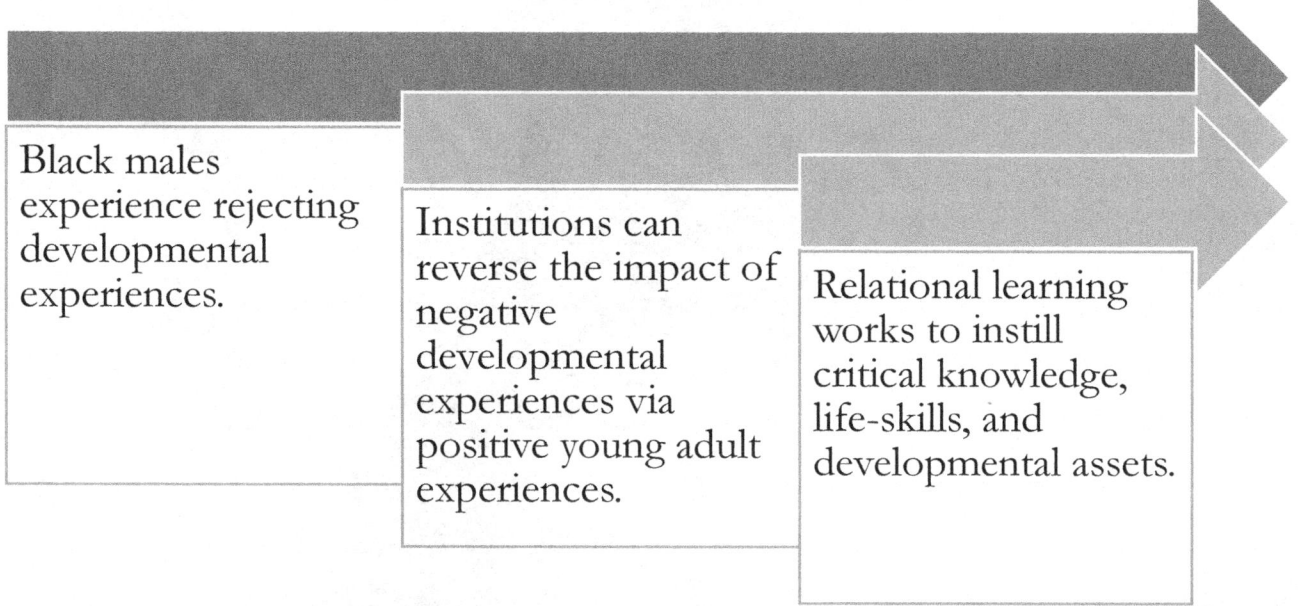

Black males have unique social experiences which in turn produce unique psychological experiences. These unique psychological experiences generate unique educational needs that ultimately require unique mentoring approaches. A racially-considerate institution understands there must be unique and innovative components within a learning environment that is attempting to educate Black male students. These unique and innovative components should be designed to minimize the impact of negative developmental experiences on the Black male student's ability to sustain productive functioning. Furthermore, in keeping with empirical data, these institutional components must intentionally utilize relational learning as a primary medium for fostering the desired developmental outcomes of both the institution and the student.

GOLDEN RULE 19

The Goal and Effect of Mentoring

MENTAL EFFECTS	EDUCATIONAL EFFECTS
MAXIMIZED LIVING	**MAXIMIZED LEARNING**

    EPS guided mentors are intentional about teaching their students the mental and educational steps they need to take in order to maximize their personal and professional development. Mental strategies include stress management, optimism, emotional intelligence, goal-setting, time management, relationship management, organization, money management, etc. Educational strategies include utilization of support services, securing of disability accommodations, outlining an education plan, effective note-taking, optimizing studying strategies, etc. Mental and educational strategies combine to increase the Black male student's probability of achieving academic success.

SECTION II.

The Social Engineering of Black Male Failure

GOLDEN RULE 20
The 5 Dimensions of Black Male Failure

Before encountering institutional barriers Black males enter college with race-specific life challenges, learning challenges, social challenges, and psychological challenges. These personal challenges serve as the master gears or predictors of academic failure and eventual poor life outcomes for many Black male students. Without some form of specialized/racialized intervention, this country will never witness the closing of the achievement gaps that separate Black males from all other racial subgroups. With this in mind, the EPS Mentoring Model serves the purpose of utilizing a relational learning platform is to assist Black males in the process of becoming invulnerable to racism, acquiring psychological empowerment, and accomplishing their educational goals. EPS guided mentors must be careful to consider the historical and modern-day social experiences of the Black male college student. QUESTION: What are the desired developmental outcomes of a mentoring relationship with a Black male student?

ANSWER: To build into mentees an ability to exert a will and resilience stronger than their environmental challenges.

GOLDEN RULE 21
Consideration is Revelation

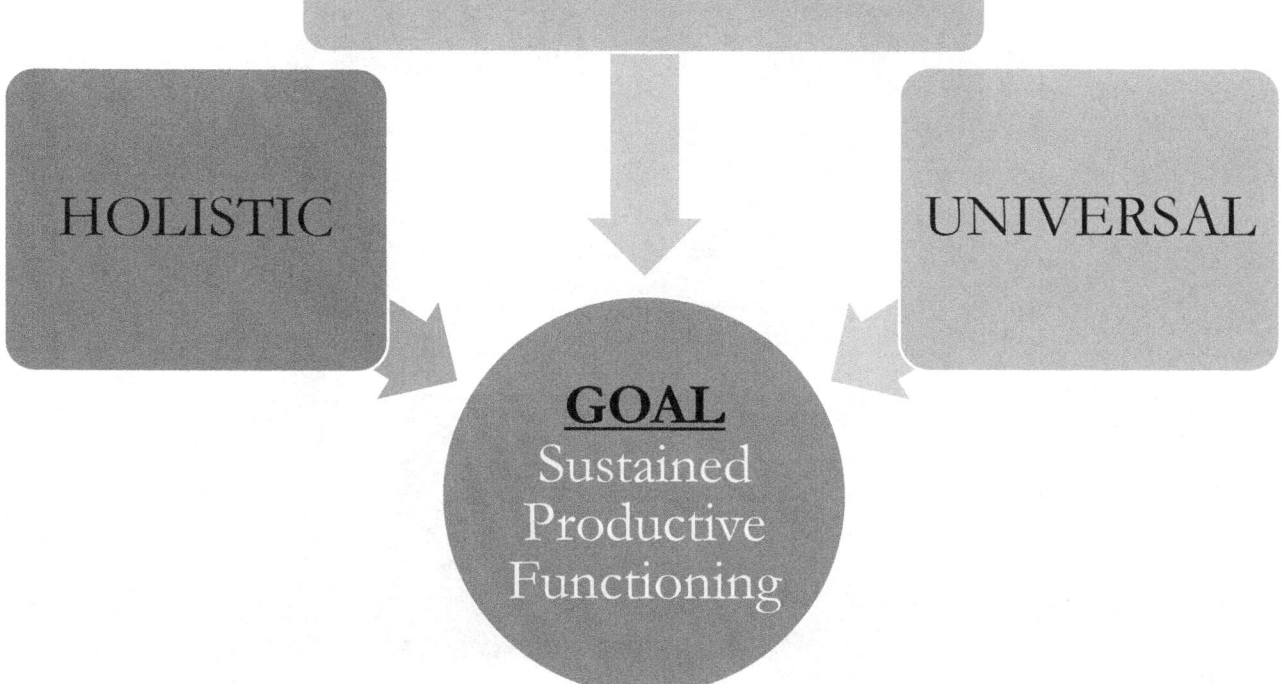

In order for any institution to effectively build a learning environment that increases the capacity for Black male learning, there has to be an intentional consideration of the multiple aspects that make-up the Black male college experience. This global consideration can empower an institution in its efforts to help their Black male students outmaneuver the institutional, learning, life, social, and psychological barriers they face on a day-to-day-basis.

Without this intentional holistic consideration, the possibility of an institution improving the academic performance of its Black male student is drastically decreased. Institutions are functioning in a holistically considerate manner when they strategically provide Black male students with a racially-contextualized curriculum (information, instructions, ideas, people, support, resources, social networks, etc.) that will effectively foster optimal levels of personal, social, educational, and professional development.

GOLDEN RULE 22
The Social Engineering of Black Male Failure

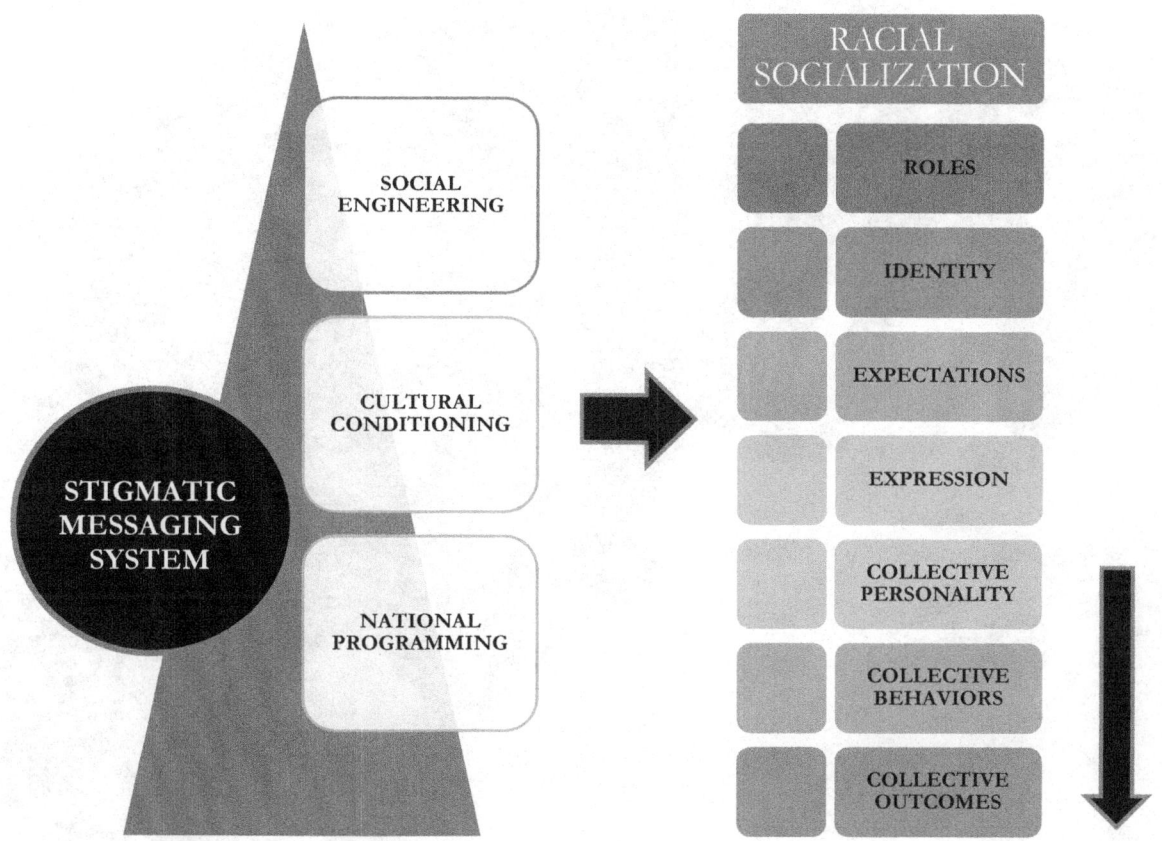

The purpose of National Stigma is to use dehumanizing messages, interactions, ideals, and images to negatively characterize the internal assets of a specific race of people. This stigmatic categorization leads to the assigning of the stigmatized racial group to a lower, inferior, and irrelevant class. As this stigmatization intensifies, the stigmatized group begins to align its thinking, feeling, and behaving with the contents of the stigmatic messaging system. As strategically intended, society also begins to align its thoughts, feelings, and attitudes about the stigmatized group with the negative messages that now define and describe the internal assets of an entire race of people. Once members of the stigmatized group (e.g. Black males) begin to identify and internalize these messages of inferiority, they also begin to align their identities, expectations, values, and beliefs with the self-limiting and socially-ineffective character descriptions placed upon their racial group.

GOLDEN RULE 23

Socio-Traumatic Experiences = Psycho-Traumatic Conditioning

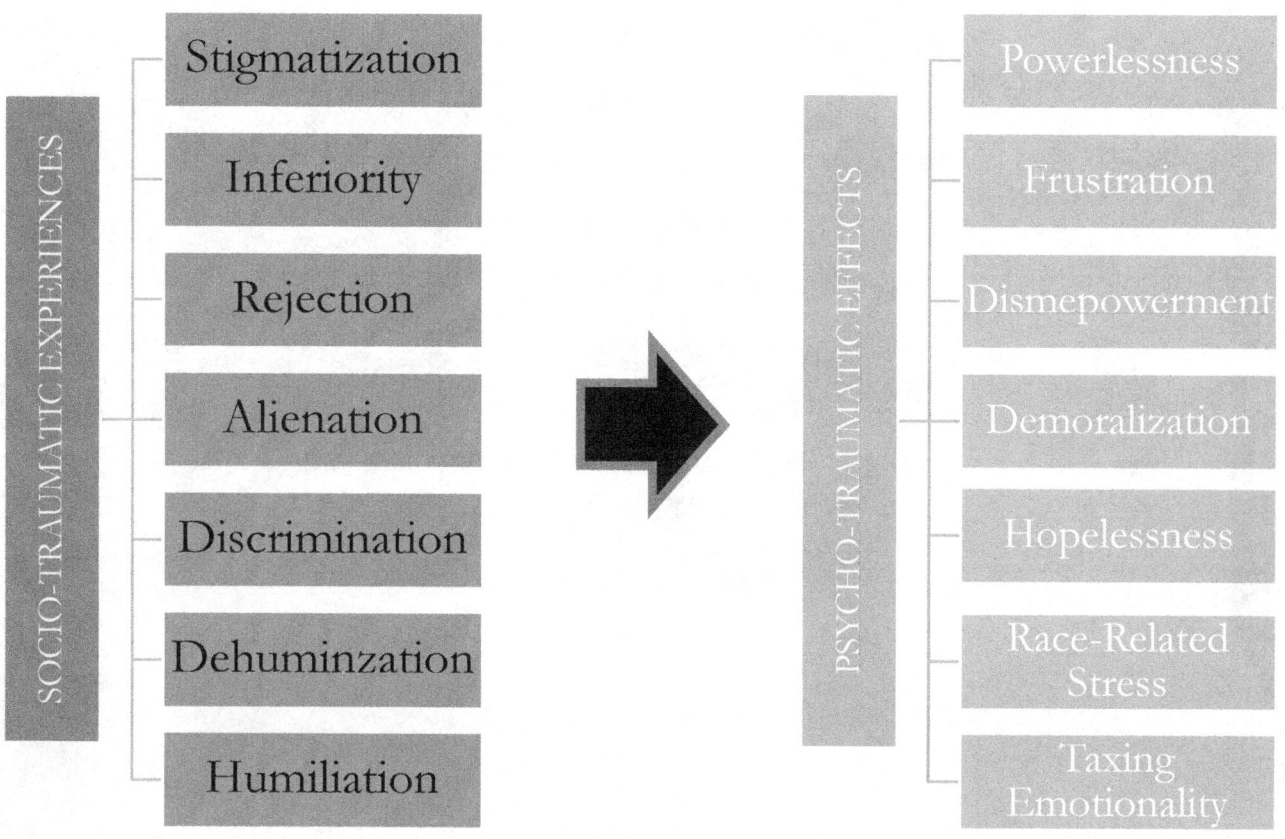

    Black males are miseducated by a social curriculum that systematically exposes them to frequent, intense, and sustained instances of mass social rejection, alienation, and marginalization. Sustained mental and emotional immersion in such a socially-abusive environment leads to the developmental experiencing of disempowerment, disillusionment, and demoralization. This form of psychological functioning ultimately manifests itself in disorganized, dysfunctional, and counter-productive behavior patterns. This pattern of disorganized, dysfunctional, and counter-productive behavior eventually leads to academic failure and poor life outcomes for many Black males.

GOLDEN RULE 24
State of Mind = State of Affairs

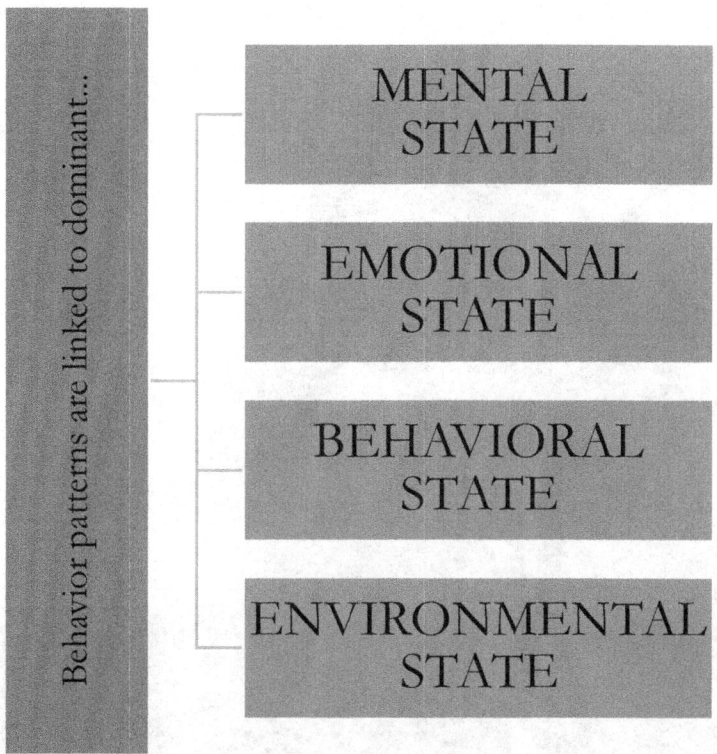

National Stigma impacts and informs the identity-forming process of the developing Black male. These stigmatic messages begin to serve as the building blocks that make-up the framework of the Black male personality. These stigmatic messages also begin to serve as a fuel energizing the emotional state of the collective Black male. In the end, these negative messages work like gloomy lenses that Black males use to perceive and interpret the people, places, things, and events that make up their lives and realities.

Once negative messaging has infiltrated the identity, psyche, and personality shaping processes of the Black male, the environment plays a sinister role in triggering the stigmatic perceptual, emotional, and behavioral attributes uploaded into the collective Black male. This stigma-triggering environment now serves the cyclical purpose of triggering negative behaviors, punishing these negative behaviors, re-triggering these negative behaviors, and more harshly punishing these behaviors.

GOLDEN RULE 25

Sick with Stigma

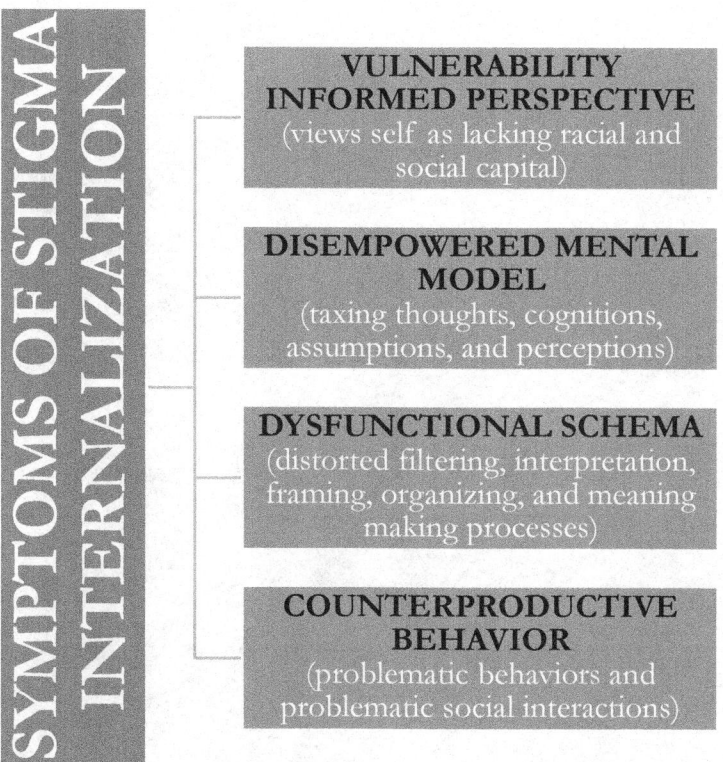

When working with a Black male student, it is important for the EPS guided mentor to identify the symptoms of stigma internalization. Black males who have internalized stigma, often manifest psychological symptoms such as automatic negative thinking, cognitive distortions, disempowering emotions, externalizing behaviors, and an overall sense of hopelessness. When engaging with these high risk Black male students, EPS guided mentors must be deliberate about re-affirming, re-conditioning, re-teaching, and re-establishing a sense of personal confidence, personal responsibility, high self-expectations, and genuine hope for the future. All of these previously mentioned states-of-mind must run parallel with a mentor who consistently challenges, supports, assists, and re-calibrates the Black male mentee. Without this constant re-calibration and thought adjusting, previous re-conditioning progress can revert back to a state of thinking, feeling, and behaving that may compromise the mentee's ability to sustain productive functioning.

GOLDEN RULE 26

You Are What You THINK!

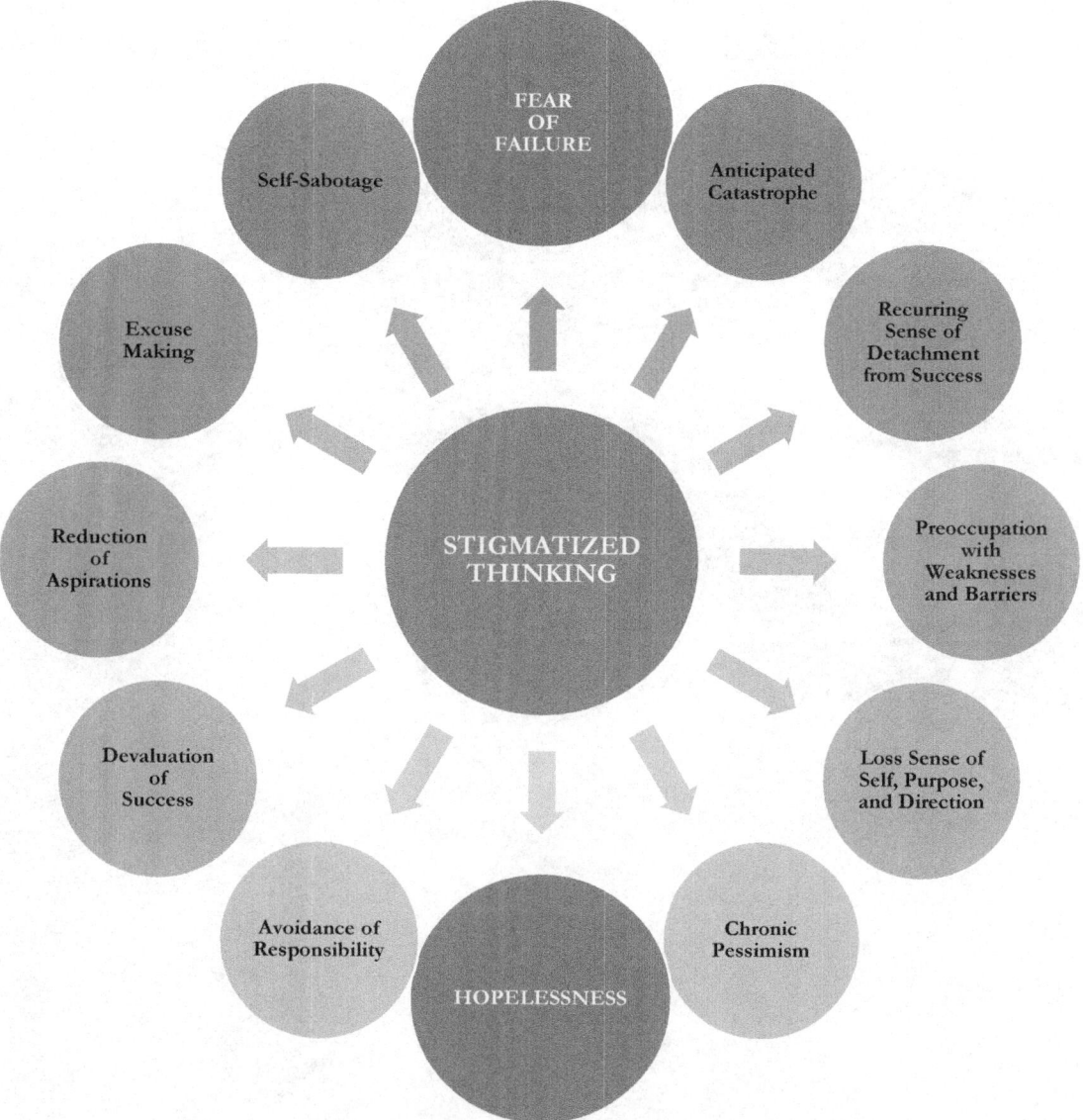

Symptoms of stigma internalization are listed above. Most of these behaviors (symptoms) are driven by the fear of failure and reinforced by a sense of hopelessness. It is imperative that mentors consistently challenge, yet relentlessly support their Black male student. By being uncompromising with a mentee's failure-driven perspectives and providing concrete evidence of hope (via your personal stories of struggle and triumph) a mentor is presenting his mentee with options for success that were previously undetected. This revelation of potential options combined with the fostering of a sense of ability re-ignites the student's flickering notion of one day living his dreams.

GOLDEN RULE 27

No Hope for the Hopeless

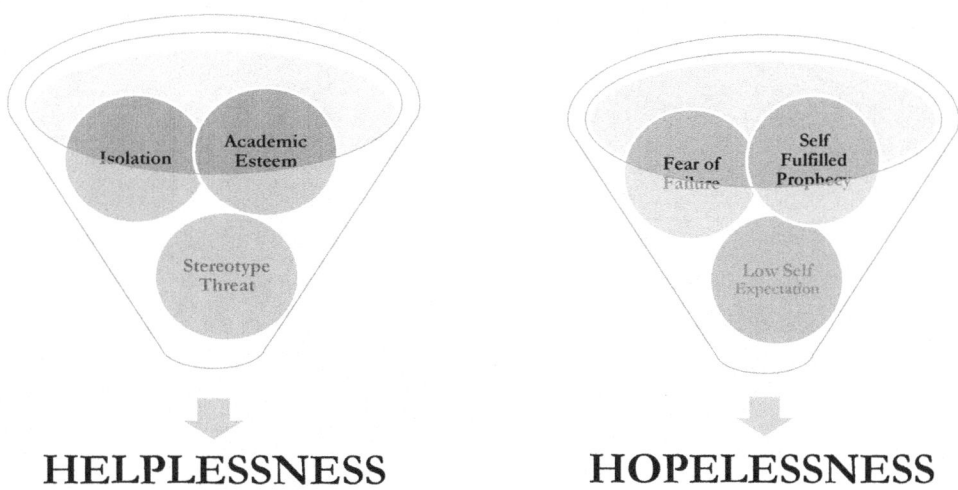

On a seemingly moment-to-moment basis, Black males are consciously and/or subconsciously aware that there is a gloomy social prophecy looming over their heads like a dark cloud. This dooming social prophecy promises an eventual state of failure. This social prophecy, like a verbally abusive parent, produces lowered self-expectations and a heightened fear of failure in the developing Black male. Such internal experiences often lead to increased feelings of isolation, decreases in academic esteem, and intensified experiences of stereotype threat on a college campus.

With all this psychological interplay taking place, social factors such as outside political and racial tensions also work to eat away at a Black male's sense of connectedness, safety, and belonging. Continued internal experiences such as this leads to a deep-seated sense of helplessness. This sense of personal helplessness and depleted self-efficacy evolves into a generalized sense of hopelessness. The two-edged sword of self-helplessness and life-hopelessness work together in an alternating manner to lull Black males away from their educational goals and towards social underachievement.

SECTION III.

How Educational Systems Fail Black Male Students

GOLDEN RULE 28

SNAPSHOT: Risk Profile of the Black Male College Student

Risks listed in White font represent risks that exist because of the student's skin color.

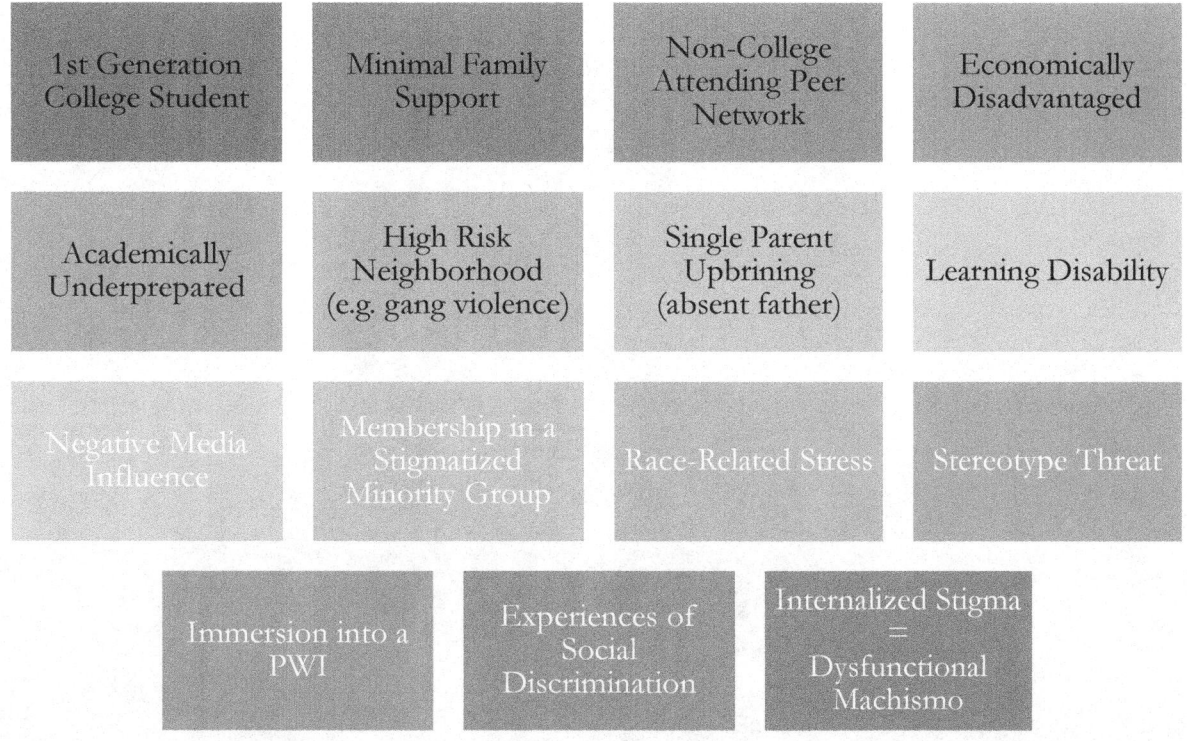

* **NOTE:** *Your institution has only 2 semesters to correct 18 years of stigmatic conditioning. After the 1st semester this student will be on academic probation. After the 2nd semester this student will be on academic suspension and will lose his financial aid eligibility.*

Black males enter college academically under-prepared, psychologically under-equipped, socially under-affirmed, and economically under-resourced. This rainbow of risk factors combine to produce a socially-engineered predisposition for academic failure. Although Black males come to college with the traditional student risk factors, their risk rate is multiplied by the addition of socially and institutionally-induced race-related risks. The EPS guided mentor must focus his efforts on providing his Black male mentee with the information and motivation necessary for overcoming race-related and non-race-related barriers to academic success. EPS guided mentors utilize guided questioning, critical conversations, and empowering interactions to transfer barrier-breaking levels of hope, wisdom, and inspiration to their Black male mentees.

GOLDEN RULE 29

How Your School Will Fail Black Males

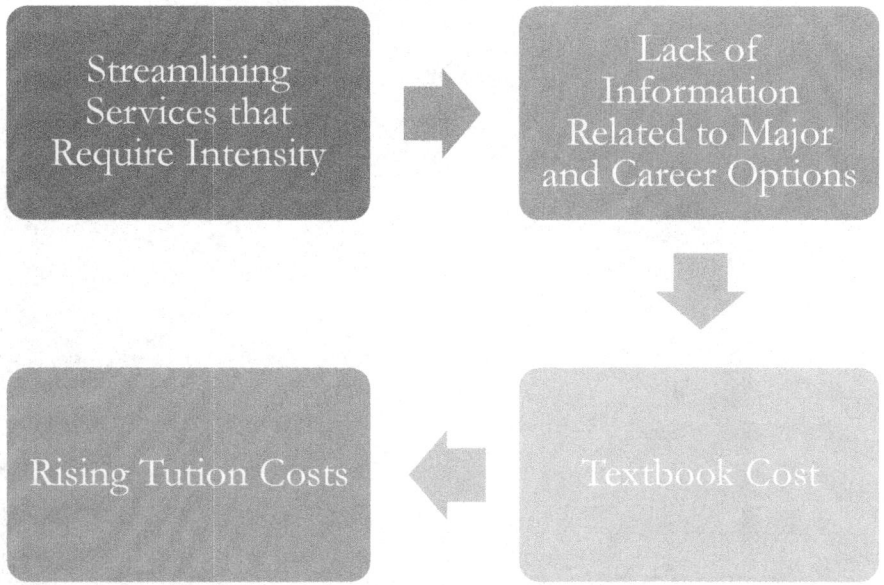

Despite institutional knowledge of the socially engineered risks Black males students endure, many colleges and universities assist (via complacency) in the sabotaging of the Black male educational experience. Due to a lack of institutional empathy and responsibility, many colleges and universities streamline student activities, events, and experiences that require greater intensity, frequency, and duration. This inability or unwillingness for institutions to expand and enhance such empowering programs and activities directly and indirectly influences the ability of all students (especially high risk Black male students) to develop the learning and living skills necessary to "do" college.

Other factors such as textbook costs, indecisiveness on career of choice, rising tuition costs, etc. come together to de-motivate, under-instruct, and/or produce economic barriers for Black male students. Such risks, barriers, and challenges can be minimized through engagement with a mentor who can fill the voids of understanding left by the school's insufficient methods of disseminating information critical for student success.

GOLDEN RULE 30

How Your School Will Continue to Fail Black Males

- Lack of Staff Diversity = Lack of *"real life"* Motivaional Cues
- Staff Intimidated by Black Male Students = Misinterpretations of Behavior
- Lack of Cross-Racial Interaction = Staff Dependence on Biases and Prejudices
- Lack of Cultural Competence = Miscommunication and Misunderstanding
- Racial Microaggressing by Staff = Decreased Sense of Belongingness

Other ways in which most colleges fail Black male students relate to the immersing of Black males into a socially intimidating setting that lacks sufficient diversity (specifically Black male staff and faculty). Black males need concrete role models or living proof that a Black male can complete the educational process and eventually attain a career. Due to a lack of human motivational cues, Black male students have a tougher task sustaining the motivation necessary to remain engaged with the process of being educated.

Other institutional factors such as staff and faculty being intimidated by Black male students coupled with staff and faculty consciously and subconsciously engaging in racial-microaggressions, leads to a learning environment that is characterized by problematic cross-racial communications. The debilitating impact of such racialized college experiences can be buffered via consistent interactions with *Black Male Mentors* who have successfully navigated similar educational experiences.

* *Note: Although rapport-building can be more complicated in cross-racial mentoring relationships, Black male students can also be effectively mentored by non-Black mentors.*

GOLDEN RULE 31

How Your School Will Keep Failing Black Males

- Blind to White Privilege
- Low Expectations
- Non Strength-Based Approaches and Posturing
- Lack of Racial Empathy and Student Advocacy

Black male students who encounter staff and faculty who deliberately ignore or are blindly oblivious to the impact of White Privilege on White American progress and the impact of Systemic Discrimination on Black American progress. Such White Americans assume themselves to be superior to Black Americans and therefore they become frustrated and impatient with their Black male students. This frustration and impatience is energized by the assumption that Black male underachievement is solely rooted in a lack of personal effort, ambition, ability, intelligence, etc.

Many White American staff and faculty have underlying hesitations and aversions towards Black male students as they perceive their academic underachievement as a lack of "social morals" instead of a lack of "psychological morale". Such White American staff and faculty verbally and nonverbally, consciously and subconsciously, covertly and overly communicate these race-based frustrations to their students on a day-to-day basis. Black male students sense these judging racial undertones in their communications with staff and faculty members. This ultimately creates a communication barrier between the student and the employees of the institution. To combat such a psychologically taxing environment, Black males need mentors who raise their student's sense of belonging, self-expectations, and overall morale. Mentors also have the potential to increase their student's academic progress by standing in the gap and taking on the role of student advocate when necessary.

GOLDEN RULE 32
Psychological Drop-Out

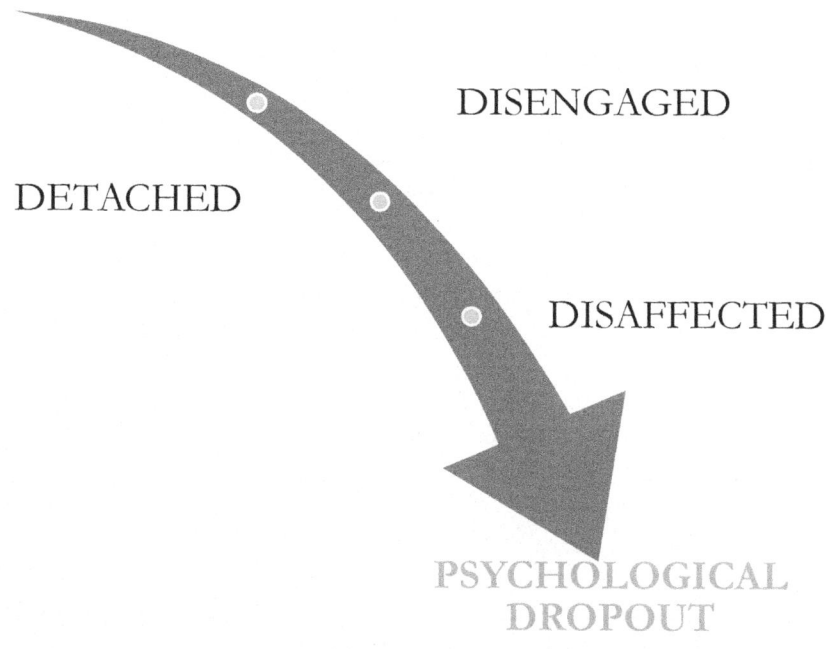

Black males leave high school mentally and emotionally detached from educational pursuits and the traditional "American Way" of achieving success. By the second month of their first semester in college, many Black males have psychologically "dropped out" even though they may still attend classes and "hang-out" around campus. Due to an intense and looming social prophecy of failure, Black males spend the first few weeks of school consciously and subconsciously looking for signs of failure.

To a Black male a failed quiz, a missed bus, a lost book, a conflict with an instructor, or difficulty understanding course material often serves as a sign(s) of impending academic failure. These disempowering interpretations of common college experiences, ultimately cause Black males to lose their focus and motivation for academic success. This loss of focus and motivation manifests itself in decreasing levels of mental and emotional engagement as well as decreases in personal effort.

SECTION IV.
The Goals and Processes of Racially-Contextualized Mentoring

GOLDEN RULE 33

A Simple Formula for Change

The concept of *Equity and Equality* is not a deep mathematical equation. Simply put, students with unique risk have unique needs. This means they require specialized institutional attention, time, human effort, resources, services, research, etc. Without institutional utilization of specialized services and resources its capacity to educate Black male students will be minimized. Institutions must embrace the "Spirit of Equity and Inclusion" by consistently engaging Black male students with culturally-appropriate relational learning experiences

These relational learning experiences must be designed to foster increased academic engagement and achievement on the part of Black male students. This increased engagement and achievement can be accomplished by using mentoring relationships to addresses the Black male college student's barriers to motivation and learning. By addressing these barriers to motivation and learning, the mentor is effectively building into his mentee a level of psychological empowerment stronger that the student's level of life challenges.

GOLDEN RULE 34

It's a tough job but…it is your job.

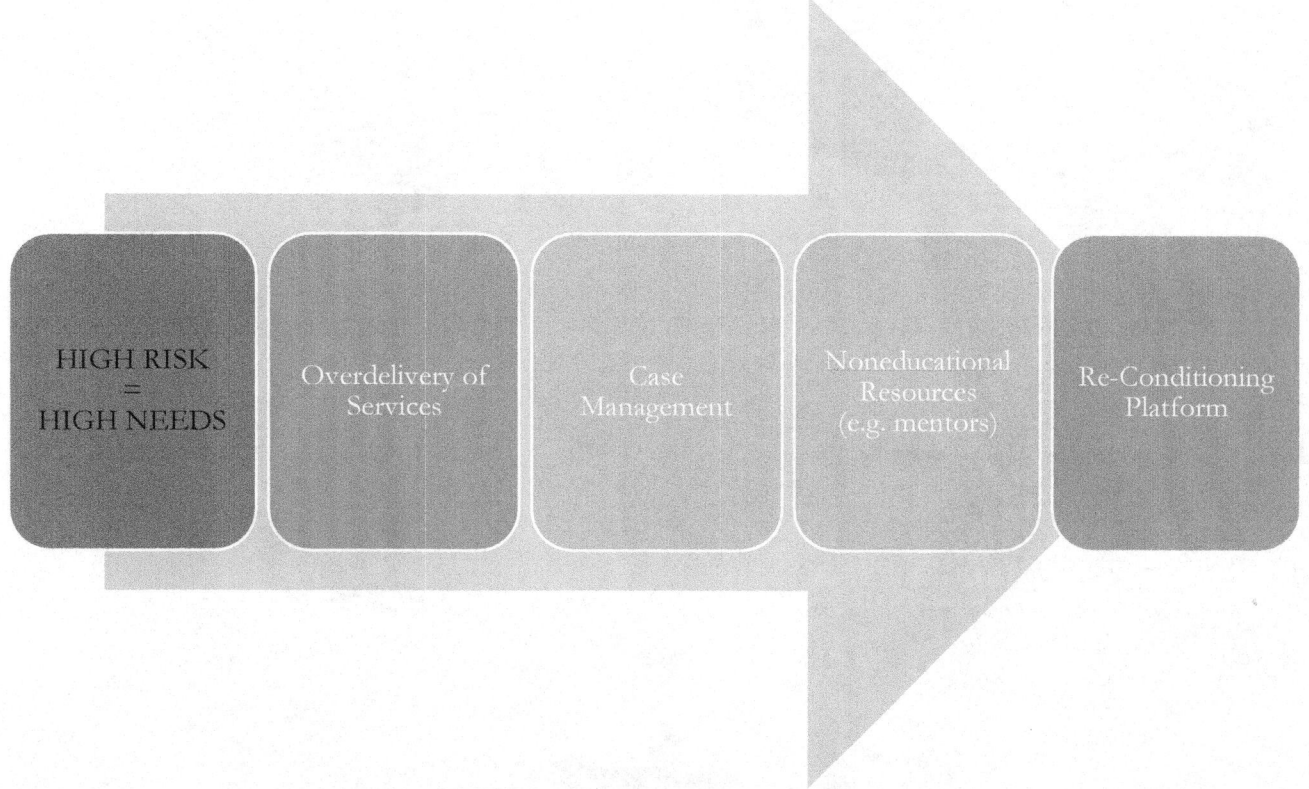

An institution that serves Black male students must understand that there has to be some level of "over-delivery" as it relates to providing services and resources. This over-delivery of services takes form in race-specific case management (i.e. monitoring, managing, and the minimizing of race-specific challenges). Furthermore, this learning environment must understand that it has to be endowed with a platform for re-conditioning the thinking patterns of the Black male student (i.e. re-conditioning = assisting the Black male student in the process of un-internalizing years of stigmatic conditioning). This re-conditioning and un-internalizing process is most effectively facilitated through the platform of relational learning. The re-conditioning goals and purposes of relational learning, although considered non-educational goals, are invaluable aspirations as they have a profound impact on Black male development.

GOLDEN RULE 35

A Balancing Act

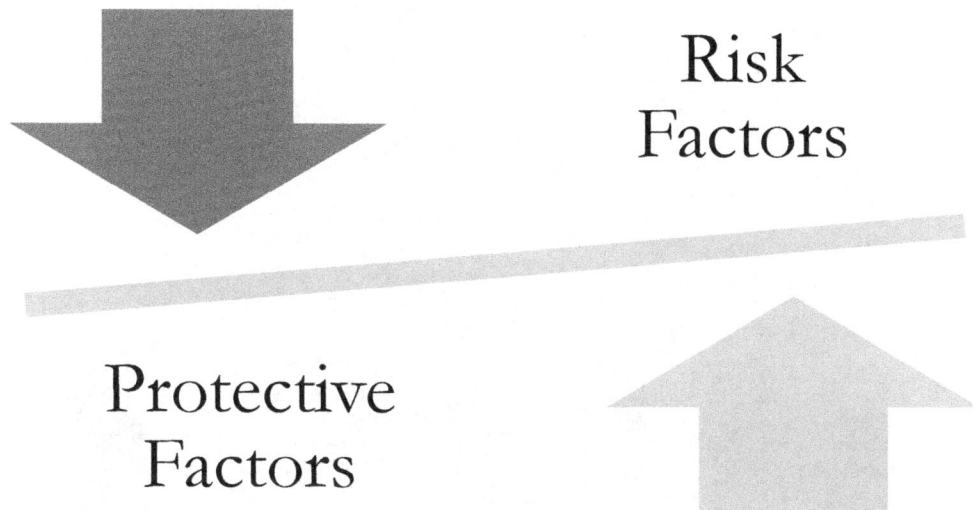

The EPS Mentoring Model views the relational learning experience as a protective factor that defends the Black male against the risks, barriers, and challenges he will most likely encounter on his journey towards academic success. This protective responsibility of the mentoring relationship manifests itself in the counterbalancing of a mentee's educational risks. EPS guided mentors serve as protective factors by assisting mentees in the process of identifying and utilizing their internal protective factors (e.g. persistence, openness, faith, optimism, hope, readiness for change, and personal responsibility).

Mentors also serve as a type of protective factor by helping mentees identify and utilize their external protective factors (i.e. relationships, resources, and services that positively influence a student's educational trajectory). Finally, as it relates to balancing risks and supports, it is critical for mentors to appropriately challenge dysfunctional expressions, misguided values, and excuse making, while at the same time supporting and coaching a mentee through the growing pains associated with change, personal enrichment, and the educational process.

GOLDEN RULE 36

Risk Management via Case Management

In order for Black males to effectively manage their education they have to effectively manage their risks. Furthermore, their support and resource accessing must also be managed. This management of risks and resources requires case management on the part of the EPS guided mentor. In order for any institution to effectively educate its highest risk Black male student, there must be some degree of case management to ensure that the student is not only psychologically empowered but also sufficiently informed and resourced. Strategic risk management through the use of case management is optimized when the student's case is managed by an individual within the institution with whom the student has developed a mentoring relationship.

In a mentoring relationship, case management serves the purpose of helping a mentor monitor the overall progress of the mentee's educational journey. Case management is a powerful tool for outlining and cataloging a student's risks, strengths, weaknesses, available resources, accessing of resources, and academic standing. Such case management provides a mentor with a longitudinal vantage point of his mentee's overall college experience. This longitudinal vantage point will provide the mentor with a big picture view that will prove to be advantageous when it comes to appropriately addressing the ever-evolving needs of the Black male student.

GOLDEN RULE 37
Guided Psychosocial Pathway

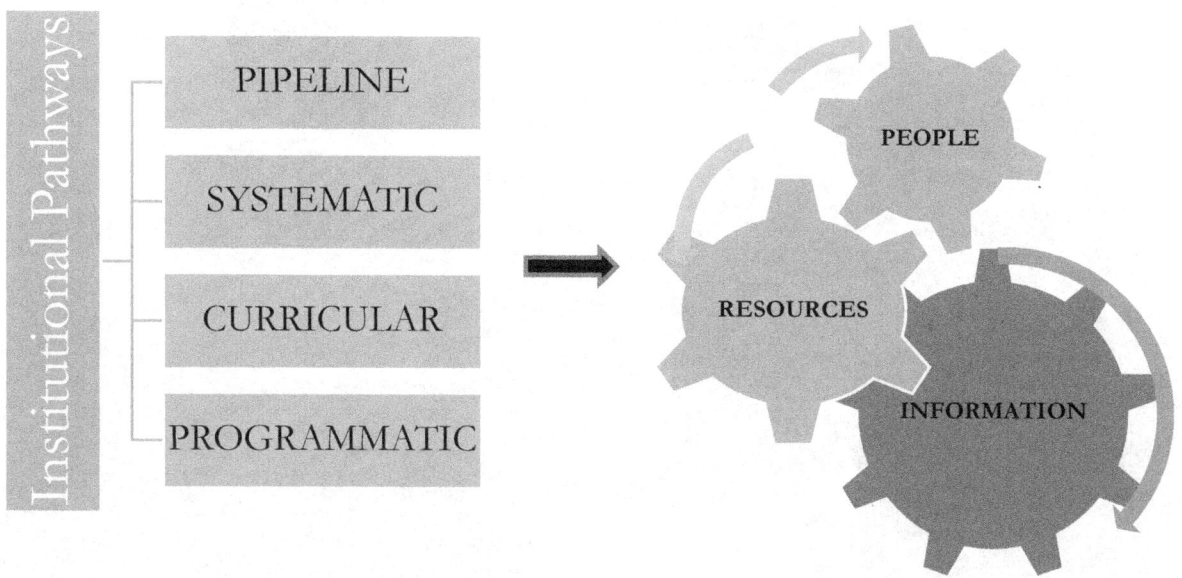

In order for many Black male students to be successful, they have to be funneled through a relational learning pipeline that is structured, racially-contextualized, and intentionally considerate of the Black male student's holistic lack of resources. This relational learning pipeline functions as a type of guided psychosocial pathway. This guided psychosocial pathway has to be structured around a specific race-based curriculum that is specifically designed to engage Black males with information, instructions, and inspiration appropriate for their personal, social, and educational experiences.

A psychosocial pathway designed to funnel Black males to the American Dream has to be programmatic and curricular in nature. It has to be a system that is driven by the gears of people, information, activities, and experiences. This pipeline of people, information, and resources serves the systematic purpose of insulating the Black male from outside institutional, political, and social forces that may trigger stigmatic thinking, disempowering emotions, and counterproductive behavior.

GOLDEN RULE 38

1 Simple goal…a psychosocial miracle!

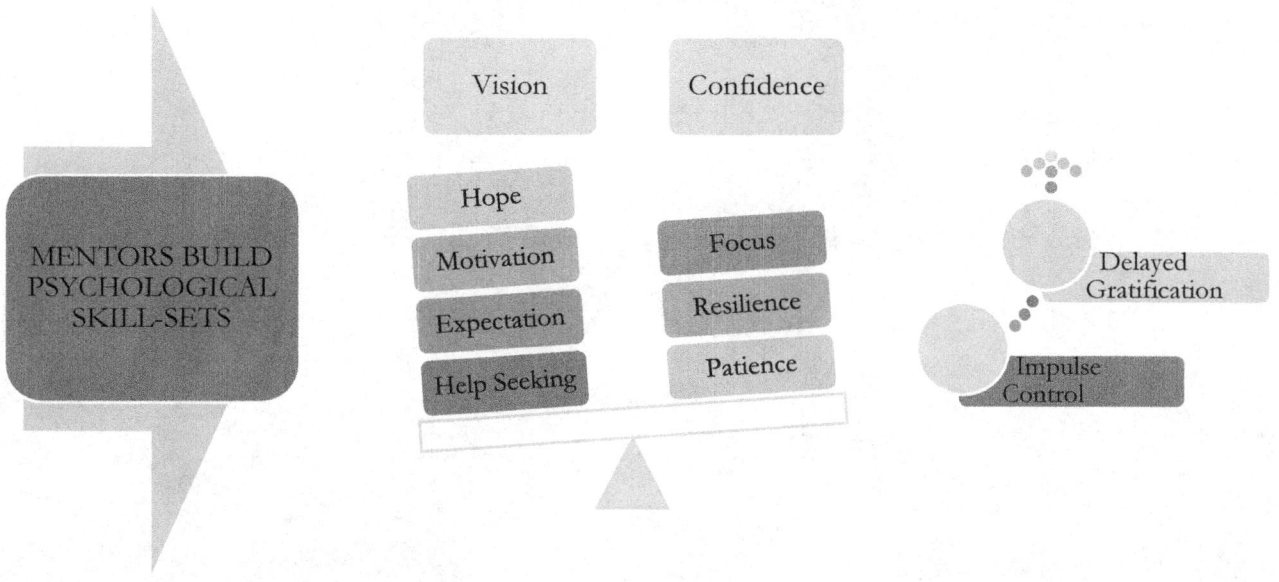

If a rejecting society can effectively work to psychologically disempower Black males, then an affirming society can work together to re-empower the Black male student. The EPS Mentoring Model utilizes people, relationships, and interactions to foster the positive mental and emotional well-being necessary for sustained productive functioning. The EPS Model for educating and empowering Black males uses the master gear of relational learning to build into Black males the psychological skill-set (vision, hope, focus, motivation, resilience, high expectations, work-ethic, etc.) necessary to thrive on a college campus. The impactfulness of racially-contextualized mentoring relationships on the morale, motivation, focus, optimism, and resilience of the Black male student will manifest itself in increased institutional capacity for educating and retaining its Black male students.

GOLDEN RULE 39

Strength Based Empowerment Capital
Protective Psychological Factors that Buffer Risks

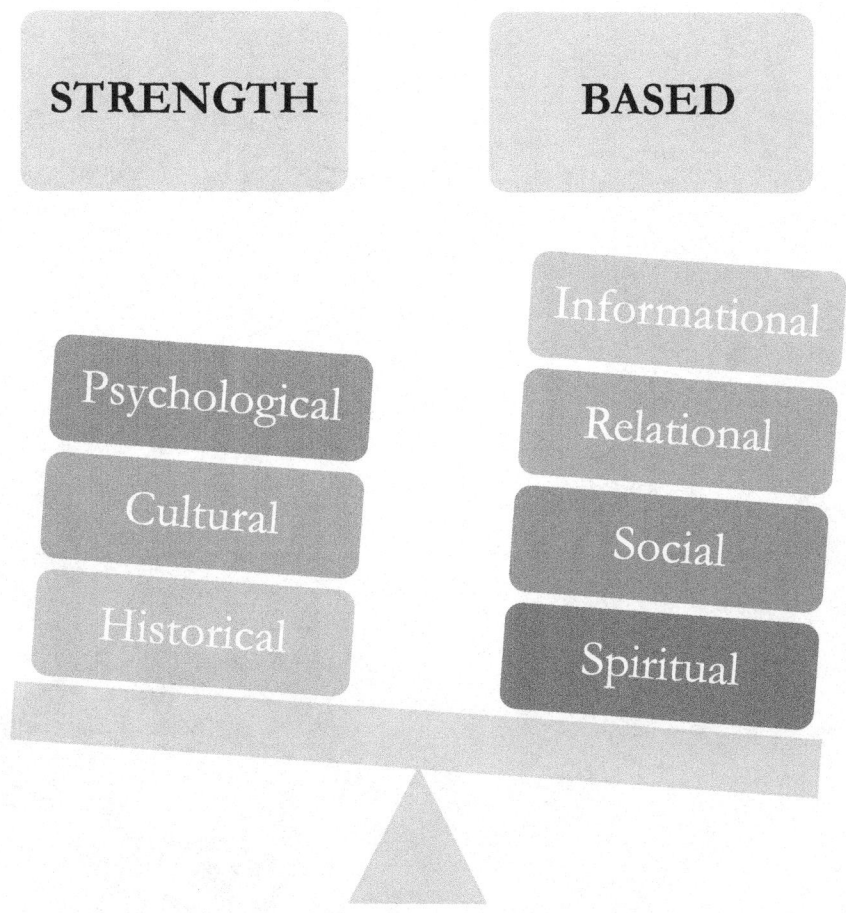

Although the EPS Mentoring Model considers the barriers and weaknesses of the Black male student, a greater focus is placed on helping Black males identify, utilize, and maximize their individual strengths. The EPS Mentoring Model also makes an intentional effort to help Black male students summon and tap into the collective strengths of the Black American race. The EPS Mentoring Model strategically integrates the collective cultural, historical, spiritual, psychological, and political strengths of the Black American race into the mentee's relational learning curriculum. These collective racial strengths are routinely evoked and utilized as a means for building mentee morale, accountability, and pride.

GOLDEN RULE 40

Skill Development = Risk Reduction

12 Life-Skill Developmental Goals

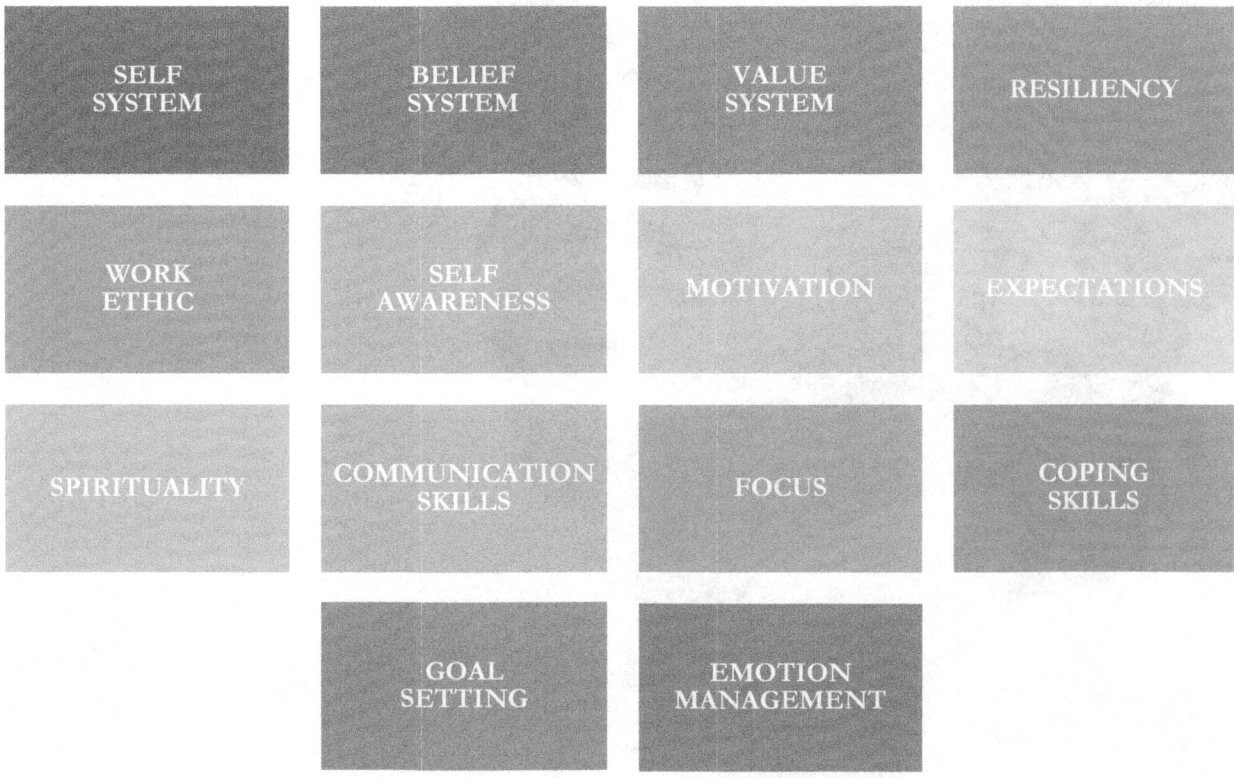

In order for Black males to successfully engage and conquer the educational process, they have to know how to *live* and *learn*. Mentors use conversational learning experiences to help Black males develop the life-skills necessary to outmaneuver the institutional, educational, social, and psychological barriers they face on a day-to-day basis. Some of these critical life skills are diagrammed above.

The crucial life-skills that a mentor will seek to foster in the Black male student include self-awareness, work-ethic, sustained focus, motivation, high expectations, good communication skills, time management, goal-setting, emotion management, etc. Although these life-skills seem basic, for Black males they can be difficult to attain as a great portion of their psychological energy has to be allocated towards managing the stress associated with American Racism, National Stigma, and Systemic Discrimination (in the community and on the campus).

GOLDEN RULE 41

Similar Appearance = Similar Experience

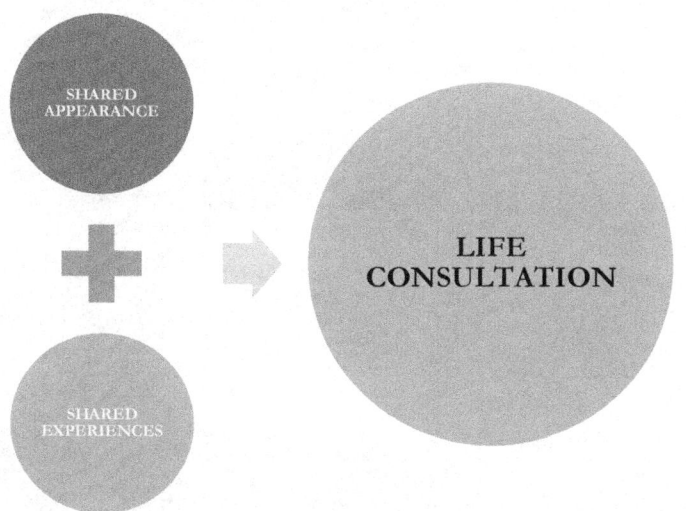

The EPS philosophy posits that Black male students will assume that Black male staff and faculty have had similar social experiences as their own. Black male students will further assume, "If this Black male was able to enroll into college, endure college, and complete college then maybe this Black male can provide me information and instructions that will benefit my educational journey".

By using Black male staff and faculty as platforms for relational learning, the institution is wisely providing Black male students with educational role-models who have shared social experiences, cultural expressions, histories, and racial perspectives. This experiencing of similar social and cultural phenomenon puts the Black male staff or faculty person in a prime position to genuinely understand and more appropriately communicate information related to the strengths, weaknesses, challenges, passions, frustrations, and struggles that are specific to Black males. This race-specific information, instruction, and inspiration is more effectively communicated by Black male mentors than mentors of other races. This is not to say non-Black staff or faculty members should not serve as mentors to Black male students. As previously stated, cross-racial mentoring relationships can be very effective at impacting the academic performance of Black males. Just note that rapport may take longer to build.

GOLDEN RULE 42

Re-Processing Life

| Re-THINKING | Re-FEELING | Re-RESPONDING |

The EPS Mentoring Model functions under the assumption that mentors are working to teach their Black male mentees how to think, learn, and understand themselves, life, and reality. This thinking, learning, and understanding must be done in a manner that brings empowerment and hope. EPS guided mentors have the job of teaching Black male mentees how to interpret and respond to reality. This newly acquired mental and emotional responding represents a psychological posturing that compels the Black male student to feel better about himself, his life, and his future. As it relates to teaching Black males how to think, EPS guided mentors should be unrelenting in their efforts to provide their mentees information and instructions that will inspire them to productively respond to the setbacks and disappointments they will encounter not only in college but over the course of their lives.

Black males are conditioned to cope with stress through the use of maladaptive coping (i.e. avoidance, withdrawal, self-sabotage, and escapism). It is therefore developmentally essential that EPS guided mentors teach Black male students how to find solutions to their life problems instead of avoiding them or engaging in maladaptive coping. The Black male's purpose for engaging in maladaptive coping is to escape the psychological discomfort associated with race-related stress (i.e. the anxiety that comes with living in a society that withholds and/or takes away resources, access, and opportunities from people of your racial group).

GOLDEN RULE 43

Small Continual Victories = Self-Sufficiency

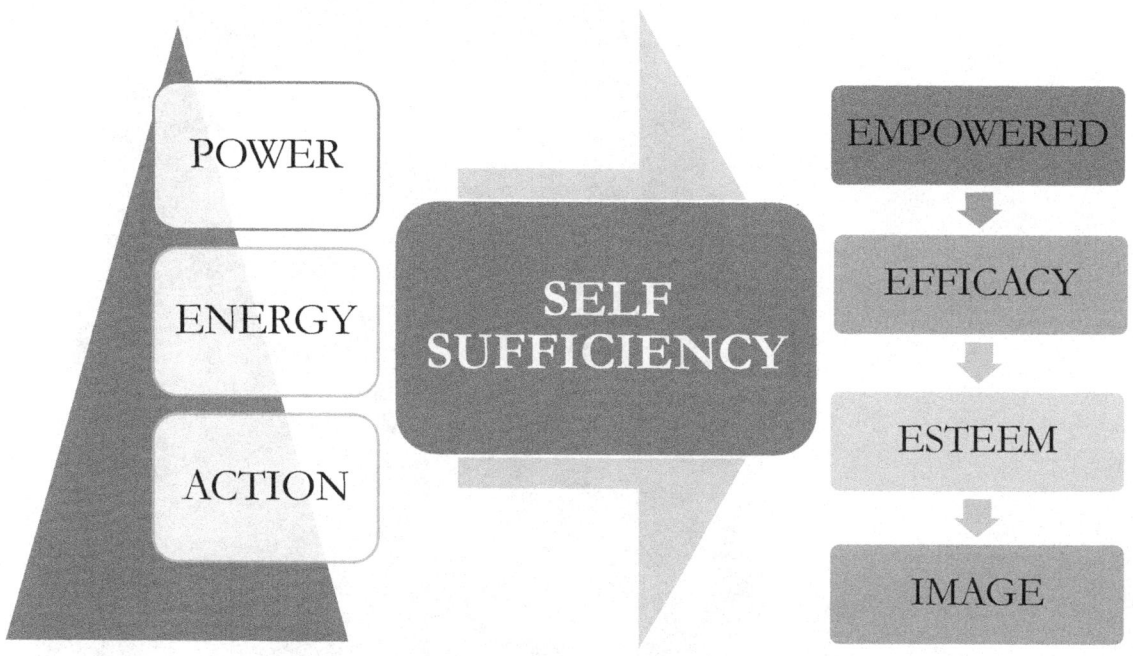

Mentors have to be obsessively intentional about helping Black males find a genuine and deeply rooted sense of power. This sense of power will convince the Black student that, "I have the skills, abilities, and talents necessary to find a place in society and acquire the things society may not want me to have". This sense of power will generate energy, which will trigger increased action, psychological engagement, and work-ethic. With this increased power, energy, and action comes the momentum necessary to "break through the walls and barriers" that have previously stood in the way of academic success. Once momentum is accumulated, the Black male student will by default experience increased confidence, hope, and personal responsibility as he now perceives himself as being sufficient enough to carry out the processes necessary for success. This sense of self-sufficiency alongside increased efficacy and esteem will help the Black male student become less dependent on his mentor for certain aspects of personal development.

GOLDEN RULE 44

Adaptive Life Processing (ALP)

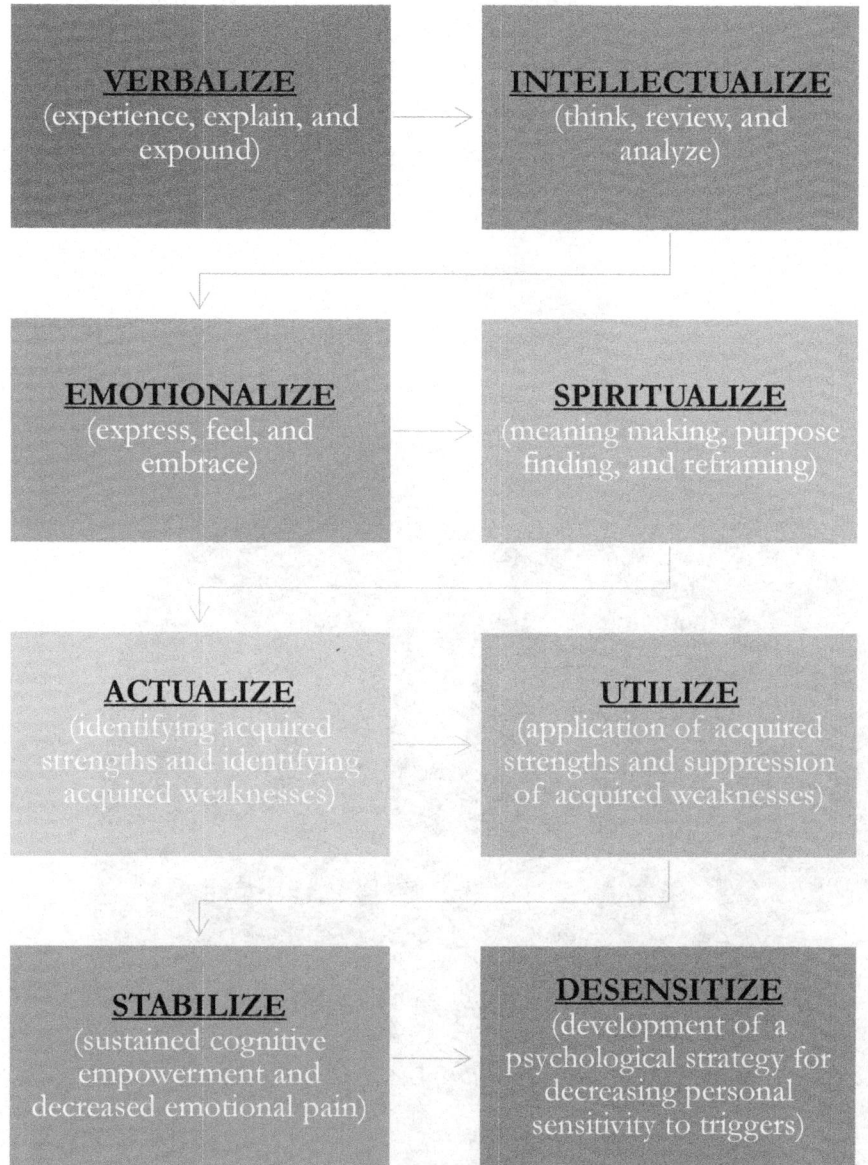

Mentors have to effectively walk their Black male students through a process of adapting to their life circumstances. This means letting go of the past, coping with the present, and preparing for the future in a way that does not lead to hopelessness. This psychologizing of life has to be done in a way that leads to increased confidence and a stronger sense of personal responsibility. The diagram above outlines the Adaptive Life Processing model for coping, framing, and responding to life hardships in a way that results in psychological empowerment. This model for psychological adaption can be used as a framework for guiding conversations between a mentor and his mentee.

GOLDEN RULE 45

Stigma Suppression Coaching

The EPS Mentoring Model places a priority on assisting Black males in the process of un-internalizing stigma and preventing future stigma internalization. Most Black males have internalized some level of racial stigma. From President Obama to the hardened criminal currently housed in a maximum security prison, most if not all Black males have internalized some level of National Stigma. What separates the Black male who succeeds and the Black male who fails is the defensive posturing he takes to protect himself from believing and internalizing the negative attitudes and beliefs society propagates about his Blackness. Without a means of guarding against the internalization of the social experiences that come with belonging to a stigmatized racial group - *academic and social malfunctioning are inevitable.*

SECTION V.

Identifying and Minimizing Risks

GOLDEN RULE 46
Race-Based Institutional Risks

- Immersed in a Predominantly White Institution
- Lack of Black Male Faculty = Lack of External Motivational Cues
- Racially Microagressed by White Staff and Students
- Social Aversion on the Part of White Student Peers
- Campus Social "isms"
- Low Expectations from Staff and Faculty
- Faculty Physically Intimidated by Black Males

Black males face many race-based institutional barriers on the road to academic success. These institutional barriers include being a minority at a Predominately White Institution (PWI), a lack of staff diversity, experiencing racial-microaggressions in the classroom, etc. Although some of these institutional barriers can be alleviated through appropriate institutional modifications (e.g. professional development opportunities) many institutions refuse or are "unable" to make the necessary modifications to their learning environments. As a result of such institutional stalemating, the job of the EPS guided mentor is to help the student navigate the institutional barriers that will more than likely remain for the duration of his college experience. By listening to the student's complaints, advocating for the student, referring students to appropriate services, and just being a friend, a mentor is performing his due diligence to inform, instruct, and inspire his mentee.

GOLDEN RULE 47

Environment Loads the Gun and Environment Pulls the Trigger

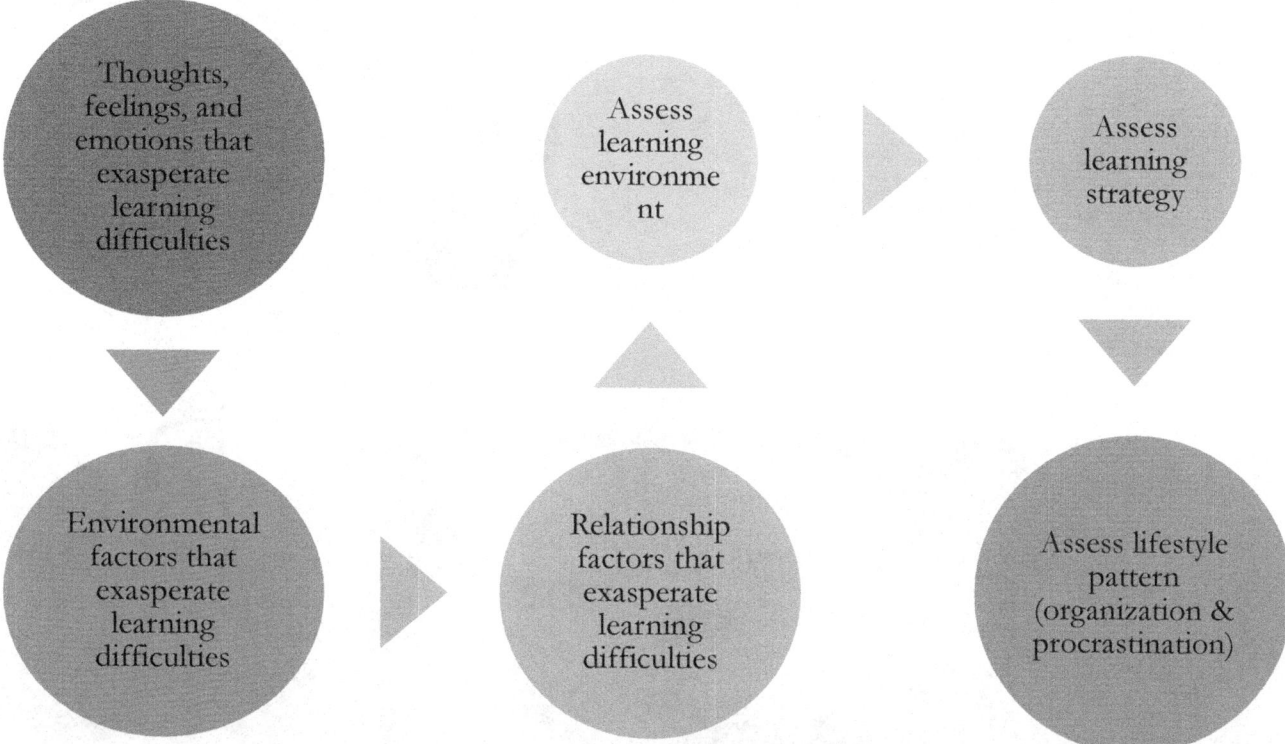

As a result of being educated in under-resourced school districts, with inferior curriculums, by under-trained staff, many Black males come to college academically underprepared. This academic unpreparedness is obvious not only to the student, but is also validated by entrance assessments that indicate pre-college levels of readiness in math, English, and reading.

It is important for EPS guided mentors to be aware that underprepared Black male students know they are underprepared. As a result of this awareness, Black male students may experience thoughts and feelings that exasperate their learning difficulties. To complicate this matter, Black males also understand that they are a stigmatized minority learning on a Predominantly White Campus with people who assume they are academically underprepared. Such a psychologically taxing learning environment works to exasperate the academic challenges of the Black male student. EPS guided mentors must be careful to discuss with their mentee any factors or behaviors that may be intensifying their learning difficulties.

GOLDEN RULE 48

Learning How to Learn

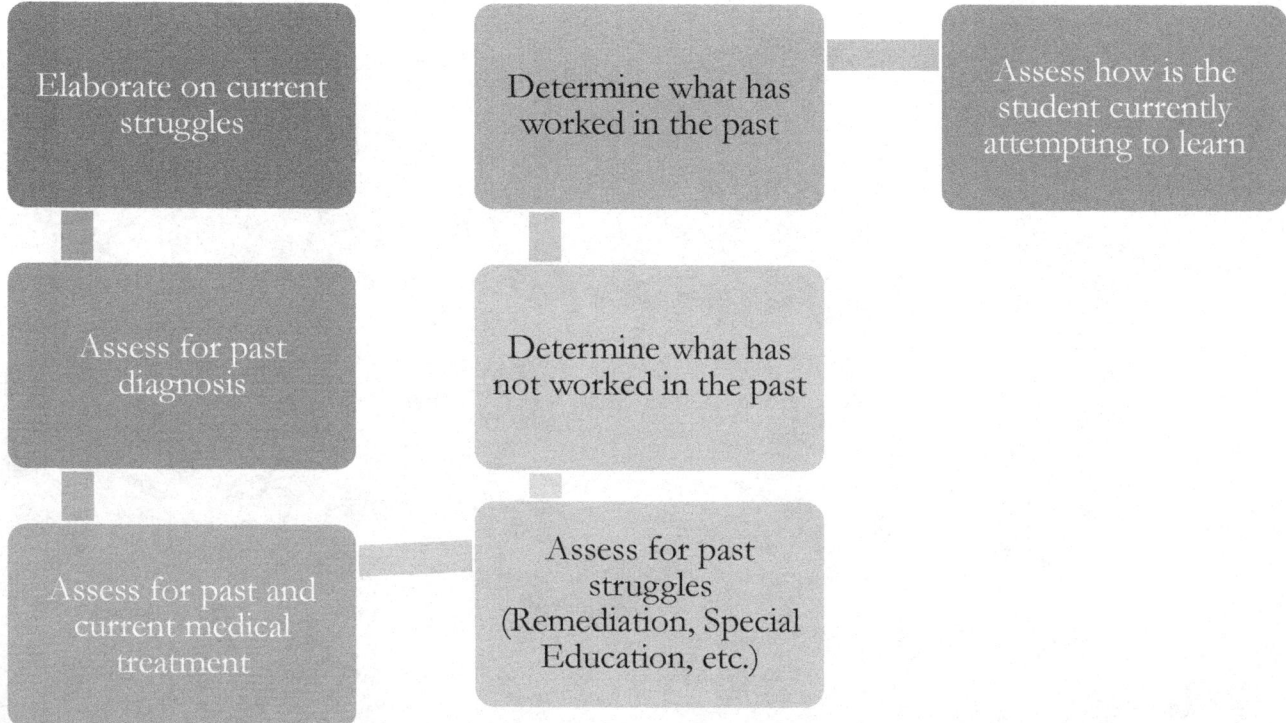

EPS guided mentors can help alleviate learning difficulties by assessing for specific academic struggles, disability diagnosis, learning approaches that have proven to be effective, and learning approaches that have not been effective. This type of assessment of learning effectiveness will enhance the ability of the mentor to help the student modify and enhance his personalized approach to learning (e.g. returned use of prescribed medications, finding a quiet spot to study outside of the home, identifying a time of day when the student is most alert, strategies for alleviating test-taking anxiety, etc.). Mentors who feel they lack the knowledge or skill-set to help their mentee develop an appropriate learning strategy should seek out consultation from the college counseling center.

GOLDEN RULE 49

Outsmarting Learning Risks - Part 1

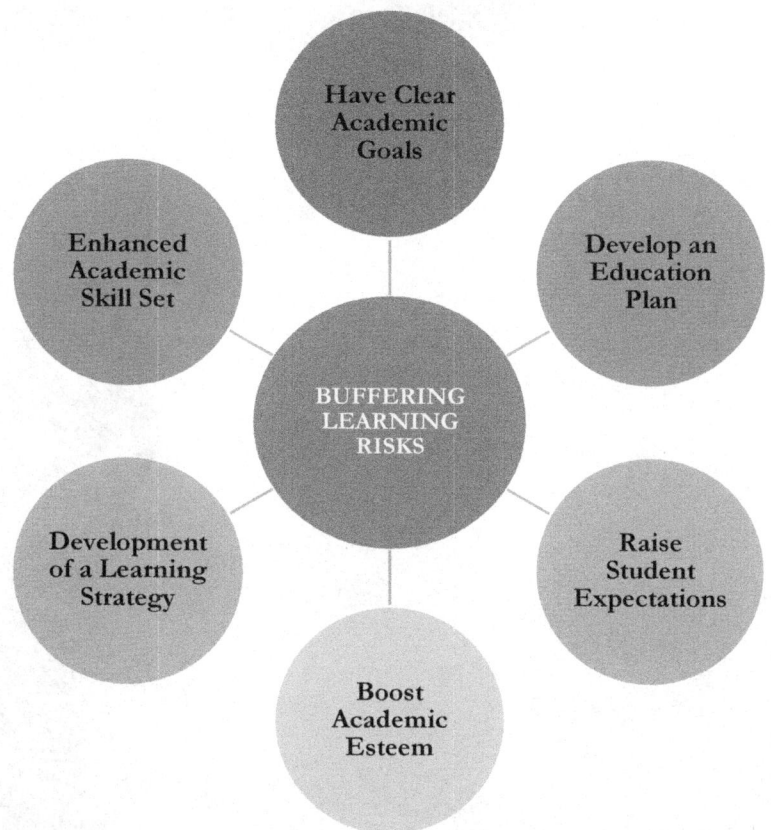

Many students, including Black males, have learning disabilities and received special services during high school. Oftentimes, these students come to college and courageously attempt take on their learning obligations without the use of their disability-related accommodations and/or medications. This endeavor is successful for some, but not for others. It is therefore imperative that EPS guided mentors inquire as to whether or not their student needs to access disability support services or return to the use of disability-related accommodations and/or medications.

GOLDEN RULE 50

Outsmarting Learning Risks - Part 2

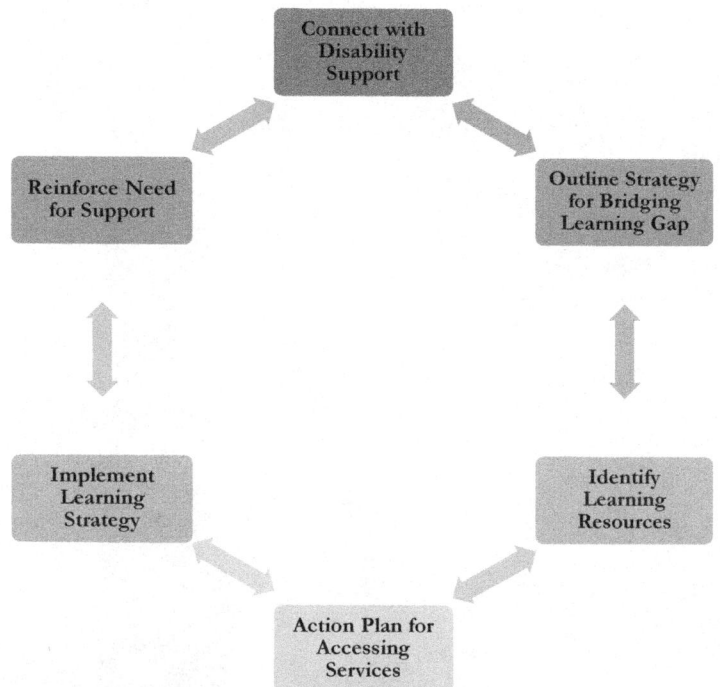

Many Black males rather they have a learning disability or not harbor low academic esteem. This is the result of not only intelligence-related social stigma but also the result of being educated by inferior curriculums in inferior learning environments. These inferior curriculums, learning environments, and social stigmas combine with the lack of a learning skill-set to disempower Black male students. It is therefore important for EPS guided mentors to help their mentees identify the various campus resources and supports that can assist in the process of developing an adequate learning strategy. This enhanced learning strategy will in turn enhance the mentee's ability to understand, learn, memorize, and recall the information they are being taught in the classroom. Once these resources have been identified, it is important that EPS guided mentors intrusively encourage their mentee to utilize the virtues of assertiveness and intentionality as it relates to accessing these resources. In many cases, mentors have to intentionally hold a mentee accountable for utilizing institutional resources identified as being potentially helpful to the student. Without this extra layer of accountability, the student may deviate from the agreed upon resource utilization plan.

GOLDEN RULE 51

In a World of Trouble

SOCIAL BARRIERS *Relational*				
No father influence	Overresponsible for family's financial burdens	Distracting issues with significant others	Negative peer influence	Non-college attending peer group

Statistically speaking, Black males enter college with a gumbo of social barriers and risks related to a lacking father influence, being overly responsible for the family's financial burdens, and negative peer influence.

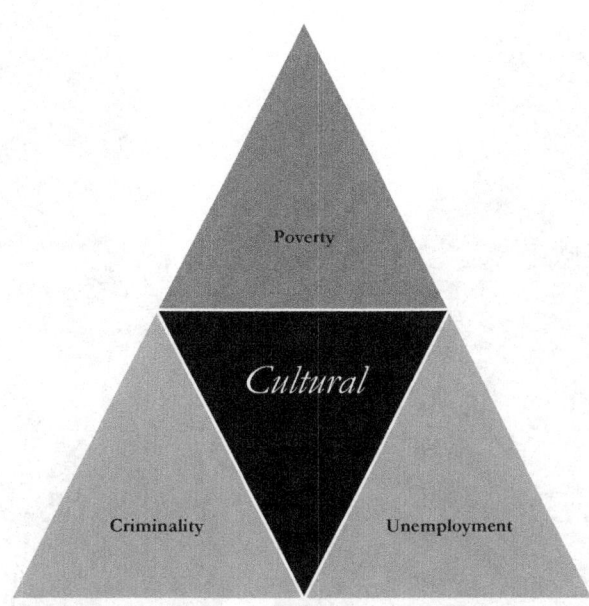

Once in college, many Black males often run into issues related to poverty, discrimination, underemployment, and criminality. All of these factors come together to create a maze of barriers that the majority of Black males never successfully navigate. As an EPS guided mentor, it is important that you communicate to your Black male students the strategies and techniques you utilized as a student to navigate financial struggles, relational issues, and other life challenges.

GOLDEN RULE 52
Minimizing Social Risks

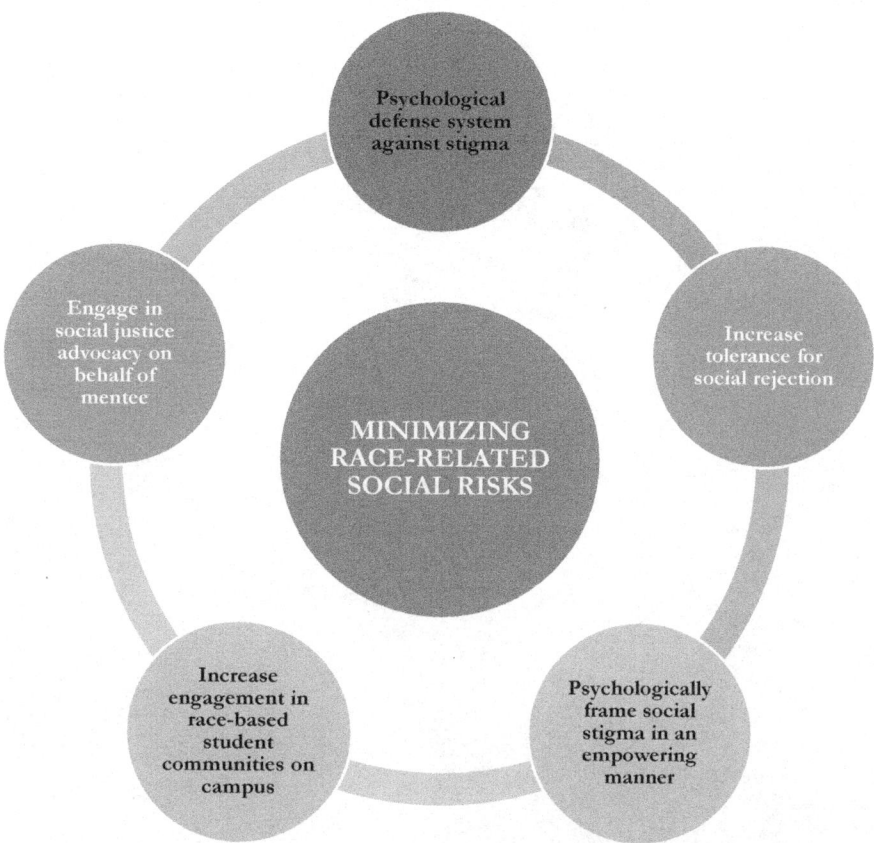

Once a student has shared their race-related social risk and barriers, it is important that the EPS guided mentor be intentional about helping the student develop a way of thinking and responding that does not make his situation worse. It is important that the mentor help the mentee identify, harness, and dedicate their strengths towards defeating their race-related social barriers. If at any time a mentor feels he does not have adequate information to empower the student, the mentor is obligated to refer the student to another mentor, seek consultation, or refer the student to other campus services that may be able to help the student overcome his social challenges. Finally, although many Black males have a culture-related aversion towards counseling, advice received from a trusted and respected mentor can do wonders as it relates to convincing a mentee to utilize counseling services as a means for productively processing his social challenges.

GOLDEN RULE 53
Psychological Warfare

PSYCHOLOGICAL RISKS
Stigma and academic underpreparedness combine to invade Black male thinking, feeling, and behaving.

- CONFUSION
- STEREOTYPE THREAT
- INTIMIDATION

- ANXIETY
- FRUSTRATION
- ANGER
- FEAR OF FAILURE
- LOW ACADEMIC ESTEEM

Black males are rarely celebrated for their intellectual abilities. In most cases they are held in a negative light when it comes to academics, intelligence, and educational outcomes. Knowing they are seen through a lens of intellectual inferiority causes Black male students to experience high levels of intimidation, anxiety, and fear in the classroom. These emotional states often sabotage the ability of the Black male to learn. As a result of this psychosocial interplay, many Black male students begin to malfunction under the stress of stereotype threat (i.e. the fear that as a Black male I may confirm the stereotypes of intellectual inferiority). Sadly and eventually, many Black males sabotage their educational aspirations in an effort to avoid the fear and anxiety they experience in the classroom. This form of escapism ultimately leads the Black male student down the path of social underperformance and an eventual poor life outcome.

GOLDEN RULE 54

Out-Thinking Psychological Barriers

- Help the mentee productively express and process his fears of education not paying off in the long run.
- Transition the student from a state of frustration, anger, anxiety, and confusion to a state of planning, effective decision-making, and productive problem-solving.
- Help the student choose a career that will allow him to express his personality, maximize his strengths, and minimize his weaknesses.
- Boost the mentee's self-efficacy and academic esteem.
- Decrease the mentee's race-related stress via the introduction of stress and emotion management techniques.

Mentors will engage in many conversations, communications, and interactions with their Black male students. It is important that the EPS guided mentor provide his Black male student with an opportunity to voice his fears and concerns in an effort to help the student successfully transition from a state of fear, frustration, and anxiety to a state of planning, decision-making, and productive problem-solving. This level of executive functioning will require enhanced levels of critical thinking. This is one of the great beauties and advantages of the relational learning platform (i.e. Black males are provided an opportunity to enhance their critical-thinking through guided conversations with a more experienced Black male mentor). Such mentoring interactions that facilitate critical-thinking about learning, professional development, time management, etc. are aspects of American success that many Black male students have never discussed with another Black male who has already attained college success.

GOLDEN RULE 55

Still in a World of Trouble

- **PESSIMISTIC ATTITUDE/DEPRESSION** - Counseling Services
- **LEARNING DISABILITY** - Disability Support Services
- **UNEMPLOYMENT** - Student Employment Services/Work Study
- **1ST GENERATION COLLEGE STUDENTS** - TRiO Support Services
- **MINIMAL FAMILY SUPPORT** - Student Organization/Veterans Support Group
- **DRUG AND ALCOHOL ABUSE** - Short-Term Personal Counseling
- **TECHNOLOGICALLY BEHIND CURVE** Introductory Level Computer Courses
- **UNHEALTHY RELATIONSHIPS** - Counseling Services and Relationship Workshops
- **FEELINGS OF PURPOSELESSNESS** - Academic Service Learning
- **INTIMIDATED BY CAMPUS SETTING** - Summer Bridge Programs
- **CAREER INDECISIVENESS** - Career Development Workshops

An EPS guided mentor is not meant to be God (i.e. is not expected to have all the answers, solutions, and personal experiences necessary to solve all of any student's problems). It is important for mentors to understand that sometimes a mentee may encounter circumstances and situations in which the mentor will be ill-equipped to effectively address. In such cases, it is the moral obligation of the mentor to refer the student to campus or community resources that may effectively benefit the student. In cases where the mentor is uncertain about what department is responsible for assisting a student with their particular needs, the mentor should seek consultation from the director of counseling services. The chart above outlines a general list of resources that are typically available on a college campus which can assist any student in the process of overcoming life challenges.

This concludes

MENTORING BLACK MALE STUDENTS

One Step at a Time

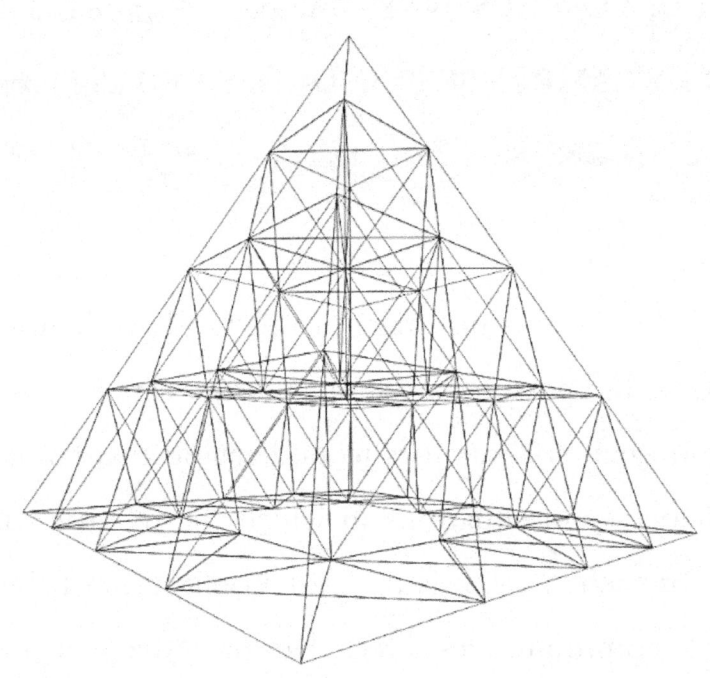

Recommended Reading

JOURNEY TO THE AMERICAN DREAM

A 21-Day Survival Guide for Overcoming Racism

This Survival Guide may be used in conjunction with the principles, approaches, and theories, presented in the 55 Golden Rules for Mentoring Black Males Students.

Made in the USA
Monee, IL
28 April 2026

49136484R00077